Triumph of the Blessed Sacrament

History of Nicola Aubry

TRIUMPH OF THE BLESSED SACRAMENT

HISTORY OF NICOLA AUBRY

Fr. Michael Mueller, CSSR

TAN Books
Gastonia, North Carolina

This edition of *The Triumph of the Blessed Sacrament: History of Nicola Aubry* was retypeset from the edition published by Kreuzer Brothers, Baltimore, 1877, and republished in 2025 by TAN Books.

Cover design by Caroline Green

Cover image: *The Vision of Saint Paschal Baylon* (detail) by Giovanni Battista Tiepolo. Public domain via Wikimedia Commons.

ISBN: 978-1-5051-3614-2
Kindle ISBN: 978-1-5051-3813-9
ePUB ISBN: 978-1-5051-3812-2

Published in the United States by
TAN Books
PO Box 269
Gastonia, NC 28053
www.TANBooks.com

Printed in the United States of America

Contents

Chapter I

Introductory

I know that there are many who call themselves Christians, and who believe in the Redemption, and yet, absurdly enough, deny the personal existence of Satan.

They assert, with an air of profound wisdom, that the word "devil," "Satan," is simply the imaginary personification of all the evil influences to which we are subject in this life. But I ask: What can be more absurd than to deny what all nations, without exception, have always believed, and still believe—the personal existence of the devil?

What can be more impious than to deny what we find asserted in plain words, on almost every page of Holy Writ—the personal existence of the devil?

Holy Scripture tells us that Satan, in the form of a serpent, seduced Eve to eat of the forbidden fruit; it declares that all the gods of the Gentiles are devils; it tells us that the devil is the prince of this world; that he goeth about like a roaring lion, seeking whom he may devour; it bids us resist the devil, and he will flee from us. St. Paul speaks of the prince and the powers of the air that besiege us, and against whom we must put on the whole armor of God, and do valiant battle.

Moreover, Holy Scripture speaks of demoniacs, or persons possessed with devils; and, among the marvelous works ascribed to Jesus Christ, is that of expelling demons, or casting out devils.

As to Catholics, there can be no question concerning the personal existence of Satan.

The Catholic Church plainly and unequivocally recognizes the existence of Satan, as may be gathered from the prayers and ceremonies of Baptism, as well as from the significance of the Sacrament itself; and not only his existence, but his power over the natural man, and even material objects. The Catholic Church has also her exorcists, and her precise forms and prayers for exorcising evil spirits.

Besides, every Christian knows that the Son of God became man and died upon the cross for no other purpose than to destroy the works of the devil, and to redeem mankind from his power.

Now to assert that there is no devil is to assert that Jesus Christ suffered so much from no motive, that His mission had no object; it is to deny the work of

Redemption. What can be more blasphemous than such an assertion?

Again, what can be more contrary to sound reason than to deny the existence of the devil? They who deny the personal existence of the devil must either deny the existence of evil altogether, which is absurd, or they must admit the existence of an unbeginning—eternal principle of evil—which is a palpable blasphemy.

No, my friends! God alone has existed from all eternity. By His word He has created heaven and earth, and all things visible and invisible. God, in His infinite wisdom, created beings gifted with intelligence and freewill, and, consequently, capable of acting wrong as well as right.

All the works of God, when they came forth from His hands, were good, very good. It was, then, by the abuse of their intelligence and freewill, it was by refusing to observe the just laws of God, that His creatures became wicked, and that evil was introduced into the world.

Satan and his hosts were created by God as bright and beautiful angels; but of their own freewill, they rebelled against God. "I will be like to the Most High." (Isa. xiv. 12.) They refused to worship the incarnate Son of God, and they were, consequently, cast out of heaven. The moment they committed that sin of pride and disobedience, they were instantly transformed into hideous demons. They are called the Princes of Darkness, of the Air, and of the World.

They differ in rank; they form a kind of hierarchy, and some are worse than others.

Their prince is sometimes called Lucifer, sometimes Belial (i.e., the Rebel), also Satan (i.e., the Enemy/ Adversary), or Beelzebub, from the chief idol of the Accaronites.

The rage, malice, and envy of the devils against man, and their enmity to all good, are implacable. Satan, the chief of the fallen spirits, makes his attacks upon men by putting on all shapes: sometimes by craft, or by snares and stratagems, as the old serpent; sometimes by disguises, transforming himself into an angel of light, and assuming the air of piety; sometimes by open assaults and violence, as the roaring lion.

He studies and observes every one's character, natural dispositions, inclinations, virtues and vices, to find out, and make his attacks on, every one's weakest point.

The natural subtlety and strength of Satan are exceedingly great, as appears from the perfection of his being, which is purely spiritual, and from examples, when God has suffered him to exert his power in a more remarkable manner. Holy Scripture tells us that the devils hurried the swine into the lake; that they killed the first seven husbands of Sara; that they have slain armies in one night; have often disturbed nature, and stirred up tempests, which struck whole provinces with terror, and ravaged the whole world.

What did Satan not do against holy Job?

He killed his cattle and his children. He covered Job himself with ulcers from head to foot.

And, in our own day, what did he not do against the saintly Curé of Ars, in France, for the space of thirty years?

Moreover, by clear proofs, it is also manifest that Satan can, by divine permission, enter our bodies, compel, as it were, the human being to stand aside and use our organs himself, and do whatever he pleases with them. But he cannot annihilate the human being, or take from the soul its freewill. It is always in the power of the possessed to resist, morally and effectually, the evil intentions of the devil. The possessed person retains his own consciousness, his own intellectual and moral faculties unimpaired, and he never confounds himself with the spirit that possesses him. He always retains the power of internal protest and struggle. Whenever this power is exercised, and there is clearly a struggle, there is no responsibility whatever of attaching to him the crimes which the body, through the possession of the devil, is made to commit. But unfortunately it very often happens that this power to protest is not exercised, and the possessed person yields his moral assent to the crimes committed by the demon that possesses him.

Such diabolical possessions have been more or less frequent in different times and places. This is confirmed by the testimony and experience of all ages, and of all nations, even to the remotest Indies. Such facts both the Old and New Testaments evince.

However, with regard to the effects of magic and possessions of devils, the Catholic Church says, in her Ritual, that such extraordinary effects are not to be easily supposed. That superstition, credulity, and imposture are to be guarded against, and that natural distempers, such as certain species of madness, extraordinary palsies, epilepsies, or the like, are not to be construed into effects of enchantments or possessions, which are not to be presumed upon ridiculous compacts and signs, nor upon vulgar prejudices and notions of the manner in which such things are done, but must be made apparent by circumstances.

The criteria of demoniac invasion or possession, as laid down by the Catholic Church for the guidance of exorcists, are the following:—

Understanding of unknown languages.

Power of speaking unknown or foreign languages.

Knowledge of things passing in distant places.

Exhibition of superior physical strength.

Suspension of the body in the air during a considerable time.

Although Satan, with implacable envy and malice, studies to disturb our temporal happiness and to compass our eternal ruin both by stratagems and open assaults, yet it is certain that he can tempt and assail us only to a certain degree; lie can go only the length of his chain, that is, as far as God permits him. This is evident from the history of Job. Before Satan was bound, or his power curbed by the triumph of Christ over him, and the spreading of the happy light and influence of the Gospel throughout the world, the empire which Satan exercised on earth was much greater than since that time. However, there can be no doubt that, in our own days, the power and influence of Satan over an immense number of men is great, very great; and it will increase in proportion as they approach heathenism and infidelity, and leave the true religion.

The Catholic Church recommends to all her faithful children, constant prayer and watchfulness against the temptations assaults of the devil. Against the mischievous influence of his malice against men, the Catholic Church has instituted, and always practiced, exorcisms and blessings. She teaches that—men being created to fill up the places of the apostate angels—Lucifer, with his associates, is permitted by God to spread his snares and exert the efforts of his malice against us, that, in these trials, we may give proof of our fidelity, and may purchase, by victories and triumphs, that bliss for which we arc created.

The following facts are so extraordinary, that many will, perhaps, doubt their authenticity. To remove, then, beforehand, every vestige of doubt from your minds, I need only state that I have in my possession a correct translation of the authentic documents from which these facts are taken.

These facts are well authenticated by the accounts published in various languages—French, Italian, Spanish, German.

They are mentioned by the most celebrated historians of the time in which they happened, among whom are—

Cardinal Baronius (wrote 1596).

Genebrard (1590), professor of the Hebrew language in the Royal College in France, and afterwards Archbishop of Aix, one of the most celebrated men of his time.

These facts are mentioned by Father Delrio, S. J., in his work on Magic.

They are mentioned by Dom Viart, in his history of St. Vincent de Paul.

Francis Frondener, in his Dictionnaire des villes (1680).

Vilette, Doctor of Theology, and Archdeacon of Laon, in his history of our Lady of Liesse.

Florimond Rémond, a Protestant historian, wrote an account of these facts. He was present at the last and most remarkable exorcism. He and his whole family became Catholics after having witnessed these wonderful events.

A lawyer of Laon wrote an account of them to one of his friends in Paris.

Goerres mentions these facts in his Mystic Theology, Vol. IV. p. 316.

These facts are authenticated, more over, by the monuments, which were erected at the time, to commemorate this extraordinary event.

There was erected, in Laon, a stone image to perpetuate the remembrance of these miraculous facts.

Also pious foundations were established to commemorate these wonderful events.

Every year, on the eighth of February, there was a Mass and a solemn procession in Laon, to commemorate the great miracle.

Also, at Vervius, a Mass and Vespers were celebrated every Thursday in the year to commemorate this miracle.

The account of these facts has been submitted to the careful scrutiny of the University of Paris, and has received the full approval of that learned body.

The history of these facts has been approved by the Bishop and Clergy of the Diocese in which they took place.

The account of these facts has been declared authentic by the most learned theologians in Rome, and has been ordered to be printed in various languages by the Popes Pius V. and Gregory XIII.

These wonderful facts, moreover, were witnessed by one hundred and fifty thousand persons Protestants as well as Catholics.

After these preliminary remarks, I now proceed to entertain you with the wonderful facts recorded in the history of Nicola Aubry.

Chapter II

Triumph of the Blessed Sacrament Over Beelzebub

Nicola Aubry was born of Catholic parents in the year 1549, in the town of Vervius, in France. She received a good Catholic education, and was married at the age of sixteen. Nothing very remarkable happened to her until November 1565, on the feast of "All Souls." On that day she went to the churchyard, and, kneeling on the grave of her grandfather, who had died two years previously, she began to pray for the repose of his soul. Whilst she was thus praying, she suddenly saw, standing before her, a man entirely enveloped in a long, white shroud. "I am your grandfather," said this strange apparition, in a solemn voice. Nicola rushed home in terror, and hid herself in a corner of the house. (Her relations, supposing that she was sick, gave her medicine, but Nicola could find no relief.) But the spirit haunted her and tormented her continually.

On the seventh of November this spirit appeared to her again, but now his face was uncovered. It was unmistakably the face of her grandfather, Joachim Villot."

"Fear not," said the spirit, "I am your grandfather."

Nicola fainted away, and seemed at the very point of death. During the swoon, the spirit told her that he had to suffer very much in purgatory, because, during life, he had vowed to make several pilgrimages, and was suddenly taken away from this life without having fulfilled his promise. He requested that her husband Louis, and her two uncles Nicholas and Augustine, should make the pilgrimages he had promised. Three of the places which he named were in France, and the fourth was St. James of Compostella, in Spain. He also requested her to have alms given, and masses offered for the repose of his soul. He then said: "Fear nothing, my child; pray to God and the Virgin Mary. You will yet behold wonderful things, for great are the mysteries of God.

Nicola recovered from her swoon, and related all that the spirit had told her, but said not a word about the pilgrimage to Spain. She then conjured those present to comply with his wishes. Her relations at first looked upon all that Nicola said as the effect of a disordered imagination; but at last they consented to comply with her request, in the hope that she would thereby regain her peace of mind.

On the ninth of November, her husband and two uncles of Nicola set out on their pilgrimage. During the journey, Nicola accompanied them in spirit. She related, to those around her, everything that the three pilgrims said and did.

Her words were not believed at the time; but nine days after, when the pilgrims returned, they confirmed the truth of all that she had said.

A solemn Requiem Mass was now offered up for the repose of the grandfather's soul, and the friends of Nicola returned from church, expecting to find her entirely restored to health. Imagine their terror, when, on their return, they found that she had disappeared. They sought her everywhere, and at last found her crouched under the bed, with her hands clinched convulsively.

Nicola at last came to herself, and related how, as she was about to go to church, she was suddenly seized by an invisible hand, hurled to the ground, and dragged under the bed. She said that she should have been killed outright, had not some higher power saved her. It was pitiful to see how the poor young woman wept and moaned, as if in the greatest agony. "Ask the spirit," said the mother, "to tell you what he wants. We are willing to make every sacrifice, in order to bring you relief." "My grandfather tells me," said Nicola, at last, "that those who have made the other pilgrimages must also go to St. James of Compostella, in Spain. I did not speak of it before, as I did not wish to give trouble to my husband and my uncles. But my grandfather says that he will torture me, and make me deaf, dumb and blind, until the pilgrimages are made."

The parents of Nicola were greatly troubled at these words, but they thought still that it might be all the effect of a disordered imagination. So they hit upon a very simple plan, which they thought would satisfy her. Her husband and her uncles came to her dressed as pilgrims ready for a long journey, and affectionately took leave of her. But instead of going to Spain, which was well-nigh impossible at that cold winter season, each went to his work as usual. The pretended pilgrims had been gone scarcely an hour when Nicola screamed out: "Oh father, Oh mother, mother, have you no pity on me? See, my grandfather says he will torture me, and wrench all my limbs, because the pilgrimage is not made." "But, my child," answered the mother, "did you not see them yourself starting on their journey?" "No!"

cried Nicola," they have not yet left the city. Louis is in his father's house sitting near the fire, and my uncles are at work."

The parents were thunderstruck. What Nicola said was literally true.

The parents now sent for the priest, and it was resolved to use the exorcism of the Church, in order to find out whether the spirit was from God or not. While they were consulting about the matter, Nicola fell into a swoon, and, on coming to herself again, she said: "My grandfather says that whoever wishes to exorcise him should have a clear conscience. He desires that Rev. F. Lautrichet should undertake the task."

The mother hastened to F. Lautrichet, and told him what her daughter had said, and begged him to free her, if possible, from this troublesome spirit. F. Lautrichet refused, at first, out of humility; but at last he yielded to the good woman's repeated entreaties. He consulted all the priests of the city, and prepared himself for his terrible task by confession, prayer, and fasting. He then went to the house of Nicola, and there, in the presence of several of the most prominent citizens of the place, he began the First Exorcism.

First Exorcism

"Who art thou?" said the priest, in a solemn voice; "speak, I command thee, in the name of God." The spirit answered through the half-opened mouth of Nicola. He spoke in a deep, hollow voice, without even once moving her lips. "I am," replied he "from God, I am from the Blessed Virgin and all the saints of heaven. I am the soul of Joachim Villot."

The wife of the deceased Joachim was present, and confirmed the truth of what the spirit had said.

"Is it then really necessary," asked the priest, once more, "is it absolutely necessary that this long pilgrimage should be made?" "Yes," answered the spirit, "absolutely necessary." "But," asked the priest, "will it not do if someone else makes this pilgrimage?" " No!" answered the spirit; "the very same ones must go who have made the other pilgrimages."

A few days after, the parents of Nicola were speaking with the priest about the great difficulty of making a pilgrimage to Spain in midwinter, and especially at a time when the whole country was in a state of revolution. The spirit interrupted them, and said: "Why! don't you know that this pilgrimage can be changed into some other good work?" "To what other good work?" asked the priest.

"Why, they can go to the Church of St. Claude, to St. Gervasius, or to St. Nicholas," answered the spirit. "Or you can have eight solemn masses offered up, seven at Vervins and the eighth at St. Nicholas. Or, better still, you can have a low mass said at St. Nicholas; and, at the same time, you must make an offering of a piece of wax. The three pilgrims should set out immediately; they will have fine weather during their journey. As soon as they return, Nicola and her grandmother must go to Liesse, and have a mass offered up for my soul. There they will see me hovering over the altar in the shape of a dove. I will bid them farewell three times, and then enter the joys of heaven. Moreover, every Friday you must offer up, at my grave, a Requiem Mass and a 'De profundis.' Of course it will not help me any more, for I shall be in heaven, but it will be of great advantage to you.

All these strange and contradictory orders gave rise to the strongest suspicions that the spirit was not, after all, the soul of Joachim Villot.

Rev. F. Lourdet, one of the priests present, said: "I can hardly believe that thou art the soul of Joachim

Villot. Art thou not, perhaps, an angel?" "Yes," answered the spirit, "I am the good angel of the deceased."

"A good angel!" exclaimed the priest, "I can hardly believe that; good angels never take forcible possession of the human body, and they do not torment the children of God." "I have not taken possession of Nicola's body," answered the spirit; "I only speak through her month. I do so by the permission of God. The saints must be served, and the vows we make must be fulfilled."

"But thou art in her body," replied the priest, "since thou speakest through her mouth. What thou sayest about serving the saints, is false. They do not seek their own honor, they desire only the honor of God. It is clear, then, that thou art not the soul of Joachim Villot, nor his good angel, but that thou art an evil spirit—a demon of hell."

The spirit was silent, and Nicola fainted away.

De Motta

The priests of the city consulted together once more; at last they resolved to send for a learned and holy missionary, named de Motta. They requested him to exorcise the spirit. De Motta inquired into all the particulars of the case, obtained from the Vicar-General full powers to employ the exorcisms of the Church, and came to Vervins on the twenty-sixth of November. Next morning, he went to the house of Nicola. As soon as he entered, the poor woman was instantly tormented by the spirit. Six strong men were scarcely able to hold her down. Father de Motta began the exorcism in Latin, but the spirit would not answer. The priest then said in French: "I command thee, in the name of the living God, to tell me who thou art."

"I am the good angel of Joachim Villot," answered the spirit. "No," said the priest, "thou first saidst that thou wert the grandfather of Nicola, but that is false, for one body does not take possession of another. Thou then saidst that thou wert the soul of Joachim Villot, but that is also false, for a human soul never takes possession of the body of another. Thou next saidst that thou wert the good angel of Joachim Villot, but this again is false, for good angels do not take possession of the bodies of men to torture them, as thou hast done. Thou art, then, neither a human soul nor an angel, but a lying spirit, a demon of hell."

"I am not in her body," replied the spirit, "I am only near her."

"Thou liest," said the priest; "thou art really in her body, and thou tormentest her. I adjure thee, then, by these holy gospels"—here the priest laid his hands upon the holy book—"confess the truth; thou art a demon of hell."

The evil spirit was silent. He was found out at last. It was really the devil.

Nicola again fell into a swoon.

Satan Unmasked

A few days after, someone, unknown to Nicola, sprinkled her bed with holy water. Immediately Nicola sat upright, and made one thousand crosses upon her shoulders, her breast, and upon every place which the holy water had touched. Someone gave her a rosary. She recited it with the greatest apparent devotion. She then arranged it in the shape of a cross, and the rosary stood upright with out any visible aid. She then placed the rosary around her neck, and no human power could take it away.

This was the last effort of Satan to disguise himself and gain credit, but the exorcisms of the Church at last forced him to throw off the mask.

On the thirtieth of November, Nicola was walking all alone in her father's garden. Suddenly a horrid black spectre (goblin) stood before her.

"Aha!" cried he, gnashing his teeth and grinning horribly. "Look at me! Am I not a nice grandfather?" He then seized her and carried her off. Her parents sought her everywhere. At last her little brother, who was only three years old, pointed to the top of the garden-wall, and cried out, "Up there! up there!"

They rushed into the garden, but Nicola was not to be seen. At length the father, in despair, burst open a small door that was firmly bolted on the inside, and there, on the brink of a deep pit, he found his daughter. She was still and cold as a block of marble.

At another time, whilst Nicola was in a swoon or lethargy, those around her heard her speaking to the spirit. "What!" she cried, "give thee a lock of my hair? No! never! A piece of my clothes? No, I cannot. Some of my father's corn? No, it does not belong to me. A piece of the window-glass? No! no! I will give thee nothing—nothing. I will make no compact with thee."

On coming to herself, Nicola said that a horrid black man had appeared to her. She was now fully convinced that the spirit who appeared to her so often was not her grandfather, but the devil himself. She was, then, really possessed of the devil; but she always struggled, like a martyr, against all his wicked suggestions.

On the first of December Nicola was walking up and down the room in which her husband was working. Suddenly she turned to him, and said: "Louis, do you not hear my little brother crying? Go and see what's the matter."

Louis, knowing the tricks of Satan, walked backwards to the neighboring room, without ever once taking his eyes off his wife. He glanced for an instant towards the cradle in which the child was lying; and, when he turned round, his wife had disappeared. Her friends and relatives looked for her everywhere, high and low, but she was not to be found. At last one of the neighbors, who had gone up stairs, threw open a door which was bolted on the outside, and there he found Nicola, crouching in a corner of the room. The demon had carried her thither through the chimney, and yet she bore not the least mark or stain of her strange journey.

On the second of December, Nicola asked for a drink. Her husband gave her a glass of wine, into which he had, without her knowledge, poured a few drops of holy water. Nicola raised the glass to her lips, but suddenly she was seized with the most violent convulsions. Her features changed—they were no longer human—it was now the face of a demon. The glass, too, remained hanging to her lips.

On the third of December, Nicola was carried to church by six strong men. It was as much as they could do to hold her.

Rev. Father de Motta, after having fasted and prayed, began the First Public Solemn Exorcism.

First Public Solemn Exorcism

The church was crowded with Protestants as well as Catholics. Father de Motta began with the exorcisms used in baptism.

"Ho! ho!" cried the devil, in a mocking tone, "are you going to baptize me? Go on. All your exorcisms will not drive me out of this creature."

After all, it was evident that these exorcisms tormented the devil horribly.

Nicola's body twisted about like a serpent.

She then stood on her feet, and hurled her keepers to the ground. Her bones cracked fearfully; it was as if every limb in her body were breaking.

The bystanders were filled with horror; they could not bear to look upon her. Whilst the exorcism was going on, a large stone fell from the ceiling upon the head of a woman who was present, and wounded her severely. The devil laughed mockingly, and said that it was he who had caused the stone to fall. He then began to prate and titter. He turned to the Protestants, and called them his friends, his children, his faithful servants. He then ridiculed them, and said that they had, on his account, broken the oath they had taken never again to enter a Catholic Church.

Father de Motta now asked Satan: "Why didst thou not answer me when I spoke to thee in Latin?" "Because I did not wish to be known," answered the demon. "Besides, I must speak in a language which the people can all understand."

"But," asked the priest again, "why didst thou order masses and prayers to be said, pilgrimages to be made, and alms to be given?"

"Because I knew," answered the spirit, "that if I told Nicola to kill her father and mother, or to commit some other great crime, she would not obey me, and I should have been found out immediately. But I do not reveal myself until I am forced to do so. Had they obeyed me, they would have carried me in triumph on their shoulders. My business is to lie and to deceive; otherwise, I should not be a demon."

"Why, then, didst thou ask Nicola for a lock of her hair, a piece of her clothes, and the like?"

"Because," answered Satan, "I wished to make a compact with her, and thereby gain power over her soul. If she had only yielded to me a little, I would have taken entire possession of her heart. But the wretched creature would not consent, for she knows now that I am a devil."

The next day, Nicola was again taken to church, and placed upon a platform so that all could see her. Father de Motta was assisted during the exorcism by two priests. One of them carried some relics, among which was a particle of the holy cross, and the other carried the sacred Body of our Lord enclosed in the corporal. Father de Motta now begged the people to pray fervently with him.

He then recited the Litany, and read the four gospels and the exorcisms prescribed by the Church. Then, pointing to the relics and to the Blessed Sacrament, he said: "In the name, and by the power, of our Lord Jesus Christ, by the real presence of His sacred Body and Blood here in the Sacrament of the Altar, I command thee, evil spirit, to depart from the body of this creature of God!"

At these solemn words the devil raved and barked, bellowed and howled, in the most frightful manner. And as the sacred Host was brought near to Nicola her whole body became horribly swollen, her eyes and tongue protruded, and her whole face was shockingly distorted.

The priest then commanded the devil, by the power of the thrice holy God, to reveal his name. After many evasive answers, and various efforts to conceal himself, the devil was at last forced to tell the truth. "I am," he said, in a terrible voice, "I am Beelzebub." The priest, then, according to the prescription of the ritual, wrote the name of Beelzebub on several pieces of paper, which he burned in the flame of a blessed candle. Whilst he was doing this the devil howled and shrieked, as if suffering the greatest torture.

During one of the exorcisms, the priest asked the devil where he went when he quitted the body of Nicola. "I go walking," answered the spirit.

"Where have you been, then, today?" asked de Motta.

"I have been in the forest of Montreuil. In this forest there are plenty of robbers," said Beelzebub. He then mentioned the names of these robbers, and the various crimes they had committed. He also accused some of the women present of the crime of witchcraft; and, as soon as they heard the accusation, they instantly took their departure.

When he saw any Protestants or bad Catholics in the church, he told publicly all their sins, even the most secret and shameful, and then he mockingly called them his friends and his children. "Yes, yes!" he cried; "you are mine; you are my servants, and I am your master."

The impure spirit then endowed Nicola with all the charms of sensual beauty; he made unseemly gestures, uttered unclean jests, and words of double meaning. Then turning to the husband of Nicola, he said: "Ha! ha! you didn't know that I was such a fine fellow."

He thus tried to excite the vilest passions in the hearts of those around him; but suddenly, at the command of the priest, he was struck dumb.

On another occasion Beelzebub was commanded to tell the reasons why he was permitted to take possession of Nicola.

"It is now about four years ago," said the demon, "that Nicola went out walking with her little sister Isabel. Isabel wore around her neck a rosary which her mother had given her. They went to the house of a neighboring woman, (here the devil mentioned her name,) and little Isabel's rosary was stolen. When they came home, the mother noticed that the rosary was gone, and, in a fit of rage, she cursed Nicola. 'May the devil take you!' she cried. 'If you had stayed at home, the rosary would not have been lost.' From that time," continued Beelzebub, "I had power over Nicola. I often tried to steal her away, for the mother gave her to me. I often threw her down, in order to kill her. I threw her into the fire, in order to burn her, and into the river, to drown her. I tempted her to say foolish and wicked words. I tempted her to steal money from her grandfather. I urged her to steal from her parents, and she stole money, clothes, meat, butter—everything that she could lay her hands on—and then gave them to her neighbors." (Here the devil mentioned their names.)

Nicola afterwards acknowledged that she had committed these thefts. The devil then continued: "I was not permitted to take full possession of Nicola, until her husband gave her over to me." Here he turned towards her husband, and said: "Do you not remember how once, when you were very angry, you cursed your wife, and wished that the devil should take her? From that moment I have possessed her and tormented her."

"Now," said the priest, "as thou has taken possession of her, thou shalt instantly leave her; for she will confess all her sins, and ask pardon of God, and of her husband and her parents. She will also restore whatever she has stolen."

"I shall take good care that she shall not be able to confess," answered Beelzebub, "for, before I leave her, I shall make her deaf, dumb and blind." Nicola soon fell again into a strange, unnatural lethargy.

Next day Father de Motta exhorted the people to pray for the unhappy woman; he then applied a relic of the holy cross to her eyes, and instantly they were opened. He next applied the holy relic to her ears, and her hearing was instantly restored. Finally he applied the relic to her lips, and immediately her tongue was loosed, and she begun to praise and thank God with great fervor. She then made her confession, and asked pardon of her husband and her parents.

On the following week the devil again took possession of Nicola, and tortured her. On being commanded, by the exorcist, to tell the cause of this new possession, the evil spirit answered, with a look of fiendish hate: "Aha! you intend to use stronger weapons against me! Very well! I, too, will employ more powerful means against you. See! I shall call all the devils of hell to my aid!"

"And I," said the priest, "shall invoke the angels of heaven to assist me. I fear neither thee, nor Lucifer, nor all the spirits of hell!"

At these words Satan bellowed like an ox, and made the most frightful grimaces at the courageous priest. Nicola again fell into a swoon, and became deaf, dumb and blind.

Power of the Blessed Sacrament

Father de Motta tried once more to expel the devil by applying the sacred relic of the cross, but this time he could not succeed; Satan would not depart. The priest now betook himself again to prayer, and exhorted all the faithful to pray fervently with him. At last, inspired by the Holy Ghost, he resolved to expel the devil by means of the Sacrament of our Lord's Body and Blood.

Whilst Nicola was lying in the state of unnatural lethargy, Father de Motta placed the Blessed Sacrament upon her lips, and instantly the infernal spell was broken; Nicola was restored to consciousness, and received Holy Communion with every mark of devotion. As soon as Nicola had received the Sacred Body of our Lord, her face became bright and beautiful as the face of an angel, and all who saw her were filled with joy and wonder, and they blessed God from their inmost hearts.

Nicola related that, during her trance, she saw herself surrounded by a crowd of horrid black men, who held glittering daggers in their hands, and threatened to kill her. She also beheld a number of wild grizzly monsters, who threatened to tear her to pieces. Flames of fire and brimstone shot forth from their eyes and nostrils, and almost suffocated her.

Power of an Innocent Child over Satan

One morning the parents of Nicola left her alone with her little sister Marie, who was about ten years of age. Suddenly Nicola flew across the room, without touching the ground, and bolted the door. The child began to cry out, "Mamma, mamma, sister is going away!" and she caught hold of Nicola in order to keep her back. The devil, overcome by the innocence of the child, was unable to carry Nicola away. He therefore said to the little one in an angry tone: "Ha! you little hussy, will you not let your sister go?" Terrified at these words, the child let go her hold, and instantly the devil threw open the window, whisked Nicola away, and threw her upon the snow beneath. Here she was found by her parents, stiff and cold, and almost frozen to death.

On another occasion, as Father de Motta had not come at the appointed time, a priest who was present took it into his head to exorcise the devil. Now this priest had not received the jurisdiction required on such occasions, and consequently Satan only ridiculed all his efforts. Turning towards the priest, he said with a malicious leer: "Now come here, my dear; you'll play the devil, and I'll be the exorcist. Go on your knees! quick! I will exorcise you!" Then the devil repeated the words of the exorcism, and made the sign of the cross just as correctly as if he had the ritual before him.

"Adjuro te per Deum ✠ vivum, per Deum ✠ verum, per Deum ✠ sanctum," etc.—But suddenly he stopped short, like one who had been struck by a heavy blow. Father de Motta was standing before him.

One day one of those standing near Nicola, saw a large black fly in the room. It was a cold winter's day, when flies are rarely, if ever, seen. The good man caught the fly, in order to kill it, but unfortunately it slipped through his fingers, and fell on the bed in which Nicola was lying sick. Louis, Nicola's husband, tried to catch the fly, but suddenly it disappeared, and, at the very same instant, he received a blow on the cheek that made his ears tingle, and the devil cried in a mocking tone: "Aha! you'll not catch me again!" It was evidently Beelzebub himself. Beelzebub means, in the Hebrew language, the "god of flies."

The Bishop

On the third of January, 1566, the Bishop arrived at Vervins, and began the exorcism in the church, in presence of an immense multitude.

"What is thy name?" asked the Bishop. "Beelzebub, prince of devils, next to Lucifer," answered the evil spirit.

"How many companions hast thou here at present?"

"There are nineteen of us now," answered Satan; "tomorrow there will be twenty. But this is not yet all, for I see that I must call all hell to my assistance."

"I command thee, in the name and by the power of God," said the Bishop, in a solemn voice, "to depart instantly with thy infernal companions!"

"Yes, we shall depart," replied the evil spirit, "but not now, and not here. My work is not yet done in this city."

"Where goest thou when expelled by the power of the Real Presence of our Lord in the Blessed Sacrament?" asked the Bishop.

"You want to know where I go, do you? Well! last night I paid you a visit," answered Satan; and then he related the very words the Bishop had said on hearing a noise in his room.

Satan was, at last, expelled again, by means of the Blessed Sacrament. On leaving, he paralyzed the left arm and the right foot of Nicola, and also made her left arm longer than her right; and no power on earth could cure this strange infirmity, until some weeks after, when the devil was at last completely and irrevocably expelled.

Protestant Preachers

As the strange circumstances of Nicola's possession became known everywhere, several Calvinist preachers came with their followers, to "expose this popish cheat," as they said. On their entrance, the devil saluted them mockingly, called them by name, and told them that they had come in obedience to him. One of the preachers took his Protestant prayer-book, and began to read it with a very solemn face. The devil laughed at him, and, putting on a most comical face, he said : "Ho! ho! my good friend, do you intend to expel me with your prayers and hymns? Do you think that they will cause me any pain? Don't you know that they are mine? I helped to compose them!"

"I will expel thee in the name of God," said the preacher, solemnly.

"You!" said the devil, mockingly. "You will not expel me either in the name of God, or in the name of the devil. Did you ever hear, then, of one devil driving out another?"

"I am not a devil," said the preacher, angrily, "I am a servant of Christ."

"A servant of Christ, indeed!" said Satan, with a sneer. "What! I tell you, you are worse than I am. I believe, and you do not want to believe. Do you suppose that you can expel me from the body of this miserable wretch? Ha! go first and expel all the devils that are in your own heart!"

The preacher took his leave, somewhat discomfited. On going away, he said, turning up the whites of his eyes, "Oh Lord, I pray thee, assist this poor creature!"

"And I pray Lucifer," cried the spirit, "that he may never leave you, but may always keep you firmly in his power, as he does now. Go about your business now. You are all mine, and I am your master."

On the arrival of the priest, several of the Protestants went away—they had seen and heard more than they wanted. Others, however, remained, and great was their terror when they saw how the devil writhed and howled in agony, as soon as the Blessed Sacrament was brought near him. At last the evil spirit departed, leaving Nicola in a state of unnatural trance. While she was in this state, several of the preachers tried to open her eyes, but they found it impossible to do so. The priest then placed the Blessed Sacrament on Nicola's lips, and instantly she was restored to consciousness.

Rev. Father de Motta then turned to the astonished preachers; and said: "Go now, ye preachers of the new gospel; go and relate everywhere what you have seen and heard. Do not deny any longer that our Lord Jesus Christ is really and truly present in the Blessed Sacrament of the Altar. Go now, and let not human respect hinder you from confessing the truth."

Suspicious Stranger

One evening a stranger came to the house of Nicola. He looked like a simple peasant, and was apparently about forty years of age. He told Nicola's father that he knew a certain remedy which would infallibly cure her, but that he must be left alone with her for some time. The priest, hearing of this, told Mr. Aubry to have nothing to do with the man, as he was probably a wizard, or perhaps even the devil himself. The stranger, on being invited to supper, partook of some food. He then went to church, knelt before the high altar, muttered some prayers, and then went towards Nicola, who was lying in the sacristy. At first he remained standing behind the keepers of Nicola, but the priest, on seeing him, told him to come forward.

Scarcely had Satan perceived the stranger when he cried out: "What! are you here, Baltazo? What a poor devil you are! How miserable you look today!"

"Yes, I am poor and miserable," answered the stranger.

Late in the evening, this stranger went to one of the priests and offered to cure Nicola, on condition that her friends would make use of some charm, and enter into a compact with the devil. The priest rejected such a proposition with horror. "Never!" cried he; "those who make use of charms, or enter into any compact with the devil, are guilty of a grievous sin. And as for you, wicked man, I would advise you to leave this place as quickly as possible."

Next morning the stranger had disappeared. During the following night the devil scolded Nicola's husband for sending away his companion Baltazo. "Aha!" cried the evil spirit, "it is well that you have always someone watching over Nicola. Had you left that loose fellow alone with her, you would never have seen her again."

"But whose body was that in which Baltazo appeared?" risked one of the keepers.

"It was the body of a man hanged at Arlon," answered the spirit.

"But this man Baltazo ate, and the devils do not eat," said the keeper.

"What is that to you?" answered the devil, impudently. "That is none of your business."

Confession

One day, during one of the exorcisms in church, the evil spirit was chattering and uttering all kinds of nonsense. Suddenly he stopped short and grazed fixedly at a young man who was eagerly forcing his way through the crowd, in order to have a nearer view of the possessed woman. The devil saluted him in a mocking tone. "Good-morning, Peter!" said he, calling him also by his family name. "Come here and take a good view of me. Ah, Peter! I know that you are a free thinker, but tell me where were you last night?" And then the devil related, in presence of every one in church, a shameful sin that Peter had committed the preceding night. He described all the circumstances with such precision, that Peter was overwhelmed with confusion, and could not utter a word. "Yes," cried the devil, in a mocking tone, "you have done it; you dare not deny it."

Peter hurried away as fast as he could, muttering to himself, "The devil tells the truth this time; I thought that no one knew it but myself, and God."

Peter seemed to have forgotten that the devil is the witness of our evil actions, that he remembers them all well, and that, at the hour of death, he will bring them all against us, as he himself declared.

"For it is thus," he added in a rage, "that I take revenge on sinners." Peter had not been to confession for many years, and, as a natural consequence, his morals were not exactly of the purest order. He had been guilty of what the fashionable world calls "pardonable weaknesses," "slight indiscretions" etc. The public accusation of the devil filled him with wholesome confusion. He rushed into the confessional, cast himself at the feet of a priest, confessed all his sins with true contrition, and received absolution. After having finished his confession, Peter had the boldness to press through the crowd once more; but this time he kept at a respectful distance from his infernal accuser. The exorcist saw Peter, and knowing that he had been at confession, he told him to draw near. Then pointing to him, the exorcist said to the devil, "See here, do you know this man?"

The devil raised his eyes and leisurely survey to Peter from head to foot, and from right to left. At last he said, "Why! really, it is Peter."

"Well!" said the exorcist, "do you know anything else about him?"

"No," answered the devil, "nothing else."

The devil had no longer any of Peter's sins, because they had been entirely blotted out by the Blood of Jesus Christ, in the holy Sacrament of Confession. What the priest forgives on earth, God forgives in heaven.

During the exorcisms of the following days, the devil was forced to confess that he was not to be expelled at Vervins, and that he had with him twenty-nine devils, among whom were three powerful demons: Cerberus, Astaroth, and Legio.

On another occasion, the devil was hotly pressed, by the priest, to tell the hour of his final departure.

"At three o'clock in the afternoon," answered the three demons, Cerberus, Astaroth, and Legio.

"On what day?" asked the priest; but the demons would give no answer.

Beelzebub then began to howl wildly, and curse the hour when he first entered into the body of that wretched creature.

"Ah!" shrieked he, "if God would permit me, I would leave instantly; but I cannot. My task is not yet done."

"Dost thou, then, not know the hour of thy final departure?" asked the priest.

"Ah, yes! but if you promise that you will not take me to Liesse, I will leave instantly, and will not return until this day a year."

"God forbid that I should make thee any such promise," said the priest; "with the help of God, thou shalt leave this very instant;" and, taking the Holy Eucharist in his hand, he compelled the evil spirits to depart.

Liesse and Pierreport

22nd to 24th of January, 1566.—The priests now resolved to take Nicola to the celebrated pilgrimage of our Lady at Liesse, especially since the devil seemed to fear the place so much. During the journey, the evil spirit opposed them in every possible way. At one time an accident happened; at another, the horses stood still, and would not budge an inch. At other times the horses would rear and plunge in the most frantic manner. Sometimes the devil uttered the most frightful sounds—at times they were as loud as a clap of thunder. At last, by means of prayer and the exorcisms, and especially by the power of the Blessed Sacrament, all the obstacles of Satan were overcome, and the travelers arrived safely at Liesse.

Layman Exorcist

That night Augustin de Moustier, the uncle of Nicola, remained watching beside her. As he was all alone, and the time dragged on heavily, he thought he would have some amusement. So he put on the priest's cassock, took the ritual in one hand, and in the other the holy-water sprinkler, and went over to the bed in which Nicola lay quietly sleeping.

"Now come, old boy," said Augustin, laughingly, "come! I will exorcise you." Scarcely had he uttered these words when Satan, who fully controlled the possessed woman, sprang upon him like a tiger, seized him by the throat, and dashed his head against the walls, the tables, and chairs, till at length the poor exorcist, half dead with pain and terror, tore off the cassock, and rushed out of the room as fast as his legs could carry him.

"Aha!" cried the devil; "don't you know how I mauled those vile Jews that tried to expel me in the name of that God whom Paul preached?"

Satan here evidently refers to what is related in the Acts of the Apostles, xix. 13–17. Some Jewish exorcists tried to drive the devil out of a possessed man by adjuring him "in the name of Jesus, Whom Paul preached."

The devil answered in a rage: "Jesus I know, and Paul I know too, but who are you?" And, seizing two of them, he threw them down and tore their clothes, and beat them unmercifully, till at last they ran away all torn and bleeding.

First Exorcism in Liesse

Next day Father de Motta began the exorcism in the church of Our Lady at Liesie, in presence of an immense multitude.

"How many are you in the body of this poor creature?" asked the priest.

"There are thirty of us." answered the evil spirit.

The priest then sprinkled Nicola with holy water, and the devil spat upon it in contempt.

"As servant of the living God," cried the priest, "I command thee and thy associates to quit the body of this poor woman."

"No!" answered Satan, in an impudent tone; "twenty-six of my companions will depart, but as for me, 1 shall not go."

The priest then took the Blessed Sacrament in his hand, and, showing It to the demon, he said: "I command thee, in the name of the living God, the great Emanuel Whom thou seest here present, and in Whom thou believest—"

"Ah, yes!" shrieked the demon; "I believe in Him." And the devil howled again as he made this confession, for it was wrung from him by the power of Almighty God.

"I command thee, then, in His name," said the priest, "to quit this body instantly."

At these words, and especially at the sight of the Blessed Sacrament, the devil suffered the most frightful torture. At one moment the body of Nicola was rolled up like a ball; then again she became fearfully swollen. At one time her face was unnaturally lengthened, then excessively widened, and sometimes it was as red as scarlet. Her eyes, at times, protruded horribly, and then again sunk deep into her skull. Her tongue hung down to her chin; it was sometimes black, sometimes red, and sometimes spotted, like a toad's.

The priest still continued to urge and torture Satan. "Accursed spirit!" he cried, "I command thee, in the name of the Real Presence of our Lord Jesus Christ here in the Blessed Sacrament, to depart instantly from the body of this poor creature!"

"Ah, yes!" cried Satan, howling wildly, "twenty-six of my companions shall leave this instant, for they are forced to do so."

The people in church now began to pray with great fervor. Suddenly Nicola's limbs began to crack, as if every bone in her body were breaking, a pestilential vapor came forth from her mouth, and twenty-six devils departed from her, never more to return.

Nicola then fell into an unnatural swoon, from which she was roused only by the Blessed Sacrament. On recovering her senses, and receiving Holy Communion, Nicola's face shone like the face of an angel.

Tempted Gypsies

Nicola was taken to the house of a friend, where she could rest a little. While the good people were at dinner they heard a strange noise in the neighboring room, in which Nicola was lying. It sounded as if someone were choking.

They rushed in, and found Nicola half strangled, with her head buried under the pillows. On coming to herself, she cried out: "Oh, what horrible goblins were here! I saw them standing at the four comers of my bed. One of them held a hundred gold dollars in his shaggy paws, and said: 'Will you have these? Don't you want them? See, I'll give you all this money if you will promise me not to go where they intend to take you tomorrow.'

'No, no!' cried I. 'I don't want your money. I'll make no compact with you.'

'If you don't, said they, we'll choke you, you miserable wretch!' and immediately they began to throttle me, and to push my head under the pillow."

After a while the priest, seeing that Nicola enjoyed the full use of her senses, began to question her.

"Now tell me, my good woman," said he, "did you never consult fortunetellers?"

"Oh, yes!" answered Nicola; "I once went to an old woman, who was looked upon as a sorceress, in order to have my fortune told."

"And what did this woman say to you?" asked the priest.

"Oh, she said that I was bewitched," answered Nicola, "and then she stole some money out of my pocket, and when she saw that I began to cry she gave me back some of it."

We can see from this fact how true it is that the devil has power over all those who consult fortunetellers, or who make use of charms and other superstitious practices.

At about two o'clock in the afternoon Nicola was again taken to church, and when the exorcism was renewed, twenty-six devils had been expelled. But four of the most powerful demons still retained possession of her. During the exorcism, the priest asked Satan:

"Where did the evil spirits go after being expelled from Nicola?"

"They went to Geneva, in obedience to my orders," answered Beelzebub.

"What sign have they given in proof of their departure?"

"Go and look at the pine-tree that is growing before the priest's house," answered the spirit. "You will find that my companions have broken off and carried away two branches of it. They have also carried away three tiles from the roof of the church."

These signs were found exactly as Satan had said.

During the exorcism the demon turned to one of the gentlemen present and said, in a mocking tone: "What! are you here, Louis Courtier? You are a widower; what business have you, then, to be living with a widow?"

He thus revealed the most secret sins of several of those in church. The priest still continued to urge the demon, and used every means to expel him. Satan grinned at him horribly, and shrieked at him in a rage. "Is it not enough for you to have expelled twenty-six of my companions? That is honor enough for the woman of this house!" By 'this woman' Satan meant the Blessed Virgin Mary, who was especially honored in this place.

"I tell you," the devil shrieked, "that even if you remain here till midnight, even if you stay here a hundred years, I will not leave at your bidding."

"At whose bidding, then?" asked Father de Motta.

"I will not leave unless commanded by the Bishop of Laon," answered the demon, angrily.

That evening the priest gave orders that the church doors should be opened next morning at five o'clock, so that the people could assemble early, and unite with him in prayer. During the night, the devil, who hates to see the people pray, stopped the clock in the church tower, as he afterwards confessed, so that the doors were not opened till an hour after the appointed time.

Pierrepont

Nicola was now taken to Pierrepont, where one of the demons, named Legio, was expelled by means of the Blessed Sacrament. On leaving, a black smoke was seen issuing from Nicola's mouth, and the demon, in token of his departure, broke some tiles on the belfry.

Here the Calvinists, urged on by the evil spirit, tried to kill Nicola and the good priest who accompanied her; but a well-armed force came just in time, and dispersed these cowardly murderers.

Laon., The Bishop

Nicola was now brought to the town of Laon. On her arrival there the people locked their doors; no one wished to receive her into his house, for all feared that the devil might reveal their most secret sins.

At last, after long and urgent entreaties, and especially after having placed a good sum of money in the hand of the innkeeper, Nicola was permitted to stay overnight in an inn not far from the church.

The next morning Nicola was brought to church. Scarcely had she quitted the house, when the devil again took possession of her. On their way to church the devil sang and whistled, and called several persons by their names. To one of the servants he said: "Aha! you got a beating this morning, because you did not clean your masters shoes."

To another he said: "And you got a good scolding because you broke a glass." This was really the case.

The Bishop who was requested to exorcise Nicola, prepared himself for this terrible task by prayer and fasting, and other works of penance.

On the arrival of Nicola in the church, the exorcism began.

"How many are you in this body?" asked the Bishop.

"There are three of us," answered the evil spirit.

"What are your names?"

"Beelzebub, Cerberus, and Astaroth."

"What has become of the others?" asked the Bishop.

"They have been expelled," answered Satan.

"Who expelled them?"

"Ha!" cried the devil, gnashing his teeth, "it was He whom you hold in your band, there, on the paten." The devil meant our dear Lord in the Blessed Sacrament.

"What were the names of those who were expelled?" asked the Bishop.

"What is that to you?" answered the devil, gruffly. "They were my dogs, my slaves; they have no name."

"Who is speaking now?" asked the Bishop.

"It is Beelzebub, the prince of devils."

Let the other two speak also."

"They shall not," answered the proud spirit.

The Bishop then, in a solemn voice, commanded Cerberus and Astaroth to speak.

"You may talk till you crack your throat," answered Beelzebub, "I tell you they shall not speak in my presence. They are my servants, my slaves; I am their master. Did you ever see a slave speak in presence of his lord?"

"I will force them to speak," said the Bishop ; "they must obey God."

"Very well! They will obey God; but I tell you they shall not speak. I am here for that. Go on, I will satisfy you."

"When wilt thou leave the body of this poor creature?" demanded the Bishop.

"Astaroth will leave next Sunday," answered the spirit.

The Bishop then held the Blessed Sacrament near the face of Nicola. The demon writhed and howled in agony. "Ah, yes! I will go, I will go !" he shrieked, "but I shall return."

Suddenly Nicola became stiff and motionless as marble. The Bishop then touched her lips with the Blessed Sacrament, and in an instant she was fully restored to consciousness. She received Holy Communion, and her countenance now shone with a wondrous, supernatural beauty.

The next day Nicola was brought again to church, and the exorcism began as usual.

The Bishop sprinkled Nicola with holy water.

"Faugh! you filthy papist!" shrieked the devil, in a rage, "away with your salt water!"

He then grinned horribly, and spat upon the holy water. The Bishop now began to read the gospel of St. John, and the devil mocked and mimicked him all the while, and repeated the very same words, sometimes before, sometimes after, the Bishop.

The Bishop then took the Blessed Sacrament in his hand, held it near the face of Nicola, and said:

"I command thee in the name of the living God, and by the Real Presence of our Lord Jesus Christ here in the Sacrament of the Altar, to depart instantly from the body of this creature of God, and never more to return."

"No! no!" shrieked the devil, "I will not go. My hour is not yet come."

"I command thee to depart. Go forth, impure, accursed spirit! Go forth!" and the Bishop held the Blessed Sacrament close to Nicola's face.

"Stop! stop!" shrieked Satan; "let me go! I will depart—but I shall return." And instantly Nicola fell into the most frightful convulsions. A black smoke was seen issuing from her mouth, and she fell again into a swoon.

Satan's Tricks

One evening, as Rev. Father Despinois, one of the priests of Laon, was taking supper with a few friends, they all heard a loud report, as if a heavy stone had fallen upon the floor above them. They did not heed it much at first, as they thought that it was perhaps caused by the cat, or by some accident. Very soon, however, two loud, distinct knocks were given on a tin basin which stood in the middle of the floor, and the sound of whistling was distinctly heard throughout the entire house, which lasted for some time. It was Satan himself, who came to annoy the good priest. During the night this mischievous spirit broke the spring of the priest's watch, and put the wheels in disorder. About midnight two flames of fire shot up from the hearth and lighted up the whole room, though there was not a spark of fire to be found there. The devil tried also to annoy the Bishop, and the priests of the city, in various other ways.

Physicians

During her stay in Laon, Nicola was carefully examined by Catholic and Protestant physicians. Her left arm, which had been paralyzed by the devil, was found entirely without feeling. The doctors cut into the arm with a sharp knife, they burnt it with fire, they drove pins and needles under the nails of the fingers, but Nicola felt no pain; her arm was utterly insensible. Once, while Nicola was lying in a state of unnatural lethargy, the doctors gave her bread soaked in wine (it was what the Protestants call their communion, or Lord's Supper), they rubbed her limbs briskly, they threw water in her face, they pierced her tongue till the blood flowed; they tried every possible means to arouse her, but in vain! Nicola remained cold and motionless as marble. At last the priest touched the lips of Nicola with the Blessed Sacrament, and instantly she was restored to consciousness, and began to praise God.

This miracle was so clear, so palpable, that one of the doctors, who was a bigoted Calvinist, immediately renounced his errors, and became a Catholic.

Several times, also, the Protestants touched Nicola's face with a host which was not consecrated, and which, consequently, was only bread, but Satan was not in the least tormented by this. He only ridiculed their efforts.

On the twenty-seventh of January, the Bishop, after having walked in solemn procession with the clergy and the faithful, began the exorcism in church, in presence of a vast multitude of Protestants and Catholics.

"I command thee, in the name of the living God," said the Bishop, solemnly, "answer truthfully to all that I shall ask thee."

"Speak on, I will answer;" replied the evil spirit.

"Who art thou that art now speaking?"

"It is myself."

"What is thy name?"

"I have told you before. My name is Beelzebub."

"Who are thy companions?"

"Astaroth and Cerberus."

"When wilt thou depart from the body of this creature of God?"

"Astaroth shall leave today. His hour is fixed, but I shall remain."

"What sign will he give of his departure?"

"He will break one of the window-panes, and take a piece of it with him."

"Whither will he go?"

"He will go to my brave Calvinist, Captain Dandelot, who would gladly put you all to death if he had the men at his command."

"Why do you keep possession of the body of this poor creature?"

"I do it to harden my Calvinists, or to convert them; and I swear, by the Sacred Blood, that I shall yet drive them to the last extremity."

The names of Beelzebub, Astaroth, and Cerberus were now written on pieces of paper. The Bishop burned them in the flame of a blessed candle, and said: "Oh, wicked spirits! accursed of God! I here burn these names as a sign of the eternal torments to which you have been condemned; and you shall be tortured until you depart from this body." At this the demon shrieked and writhed in fearful agony. Three distinct voices were clearly heard; they resembled the bellowing of an ox, the howling of a dog, and the shrill squealing of swine.

The Bishop now holds the Blessed Sacrament close to the face of Nicola. Suddenly a wild, unearthly yell rings through the air—a black, heavy smoke issues from the mouth of Nicola. The demon Astaroth is expelled forever. At the same instant, the crash of breaking glass is heard; a window-pane is broken and carried away. Nicola again falls into a deadly swoon, and is restored to consciousness only by the Blessed Sacrament.

Calvinists try to poison Nicola

Nicola was now arrested, by order of the chief magistrate, and cast into prison. This was done at the instigation of the Calvinists, who wished to get Nicola into their power, to poison her. The chief magistrate visited Nicola in prison. He was accompanied by Dr. Carlier, a most bigoted Calvinist, together with several of the most prominent officials of the place, and some of the clergy. The Calvinist physician tried every means to discover the source of "this popish trickery," as he called the possession of Nicola, and he subjected the poor creature to the most rigid scrutiny. Nicola was evidently sound asleep. Suddenly the demon took possession of her. In a lit of raving madness, she now bounded into the middle of the room, seized the Calvinist physician by the throat, and mauled and throttled him most unmercifully. The doctor was wild with rage; he struck out right and left. He tried to defend himself with might and main—but all his efforts availed him little; he was, at length, forced to confess that the woman was really possessed.

The chief magistrate and his companions rushed into a corner of the room. They were pale with terror. They no longer doubted the terrible reality of the possession. Sometimes Nicola was rolled up like a ball, and moved about without touching the ground. The terror-stricken magistrate crossed himself again and again, and screamed out: "O Jesus and Mary, help us! Ha! 'tis the devil, 'tis really the devil. Ha! Satan! back! back!" At last Nicola fell into a death-like swoon, and was laid upon the couch.

Dr. Carlier was now determined to be revenged. He drew forth a small phial, filled with a black, offensive liquid, containing the most deadly poisons, and poured the contents into the half-open mouth of Nicola. He then drew forth another phial, containing a white liquid, and wished to give it also to her, but the priest interfered. Dr. Carlier now shook Nicola, struck her hands together, called her by name, and made every effort to restore her to consciousness, but he could not succeed.

Whilst the doctor was trying these experiments, a large black beetle suddenly appeared upon the pillow, and was visible for several minutes to all. Dr. Carlier, not being able to restore Nicola to consciousness, hurried away as fast as he could. The other doctors present then tried to arouse Nicola, and, after trying in vain for a whole hour, they all confessed that her sickness was not natural. One of the priests now brought in the

Blessed Sacrament, touched the lips of Nicola with the Sacred Body of our Lord, and instantly she was brought to life.

The poor creature now screamed out: "O Jesus, Mary! what have you given me? Oh! I'm burning, I'm burning!" She then threw up the poisonous liquid, and was instantly free from pain.

At the sight of this miracle, two Calvinists present cried out: "I believe now! I have seen the miracle with my own eyes! I will remain Protestant no longer." And they became Catholics.

That very day Nicola was released from prison. The chief magistrate doubted no longer the reality of the diabolical possession.

Every day, before beginning the exorcism, the Bishop made a solemn procession through the city, accompanied by the clergy and a large number of the citizens. During these processions the devil called many of the bystanders by name, and told their most secret sins. One day a young widow—wife of the deceased Mr. Paquot—was in her father's house, looking down from a window upon the procession. The devil, on seeing her, called her by name, and said in a tone of bitter mockery, "Ha! you vain little puppet! are you there? You've already laid aside your mourning weeds, and your husband is dead scarcely three weeks! Fie! away with you!"

During the exorcism, which took place in church, the Bishop asked of Satan, "Tell me, where wert thou last night?"

"Don't you know it?" answered Satan. "I was in the prison. The magistrate will not forget it so soon. Ha! ha! How often did he not cry out: 'Nesus!' (The devil would not pronounce the holy name of Jesus.) 'Nesus! Mary! It is Satan—back! back!' And then Mr. Carlier gave this wretched creature some medicine. Ho! ho! It was I who helped Miss Sisonne to prepare it." This Miss Sisonne was a very bigoted Calvinist; she had really prepared the medicine, and given it to Dr. Carlier.

"Of what was this medicine composed?" asked the Bishop.

"Ha! it was strong enough to poison twenty persons!"

The devil then began to mimic Miss Sisonne, and repeated the very words she had used, with the very same tone and gesture.

"I see that thou art a liar," said the Bishop.

"Yes, I am a liar," answered Satan, "but I sometimes speak the truth."

"When do you speak the truth?"

"When I am commanded and forced to do so, as I am today. When I do speak the truth, I borrow it from others."

Consequence of Human Respect

The Calvinists having failed in their plan to poison Nicola, were now more furious than ever. They threatened to put her to death by force. The good Bishop, fearing some sudden outbreak, and wishing to preserve peace and good order, resolved to stop the processions, and continue the exorcisms in a private chapel. He was included to do this especially by the request of the chief magistrate, who was evidently of a very peaceful turn of mind.

On the twenty-ninth of January, then, the Bishop began the exorcism in a private chapel.

"Art thou alone?" asked the Bishop, of Satan.

"No," was the reply. "Cerberus is yet with me."

"When wilt thou depart from this poor creature?"

"You may now say and do whatever you please," answered Satan, "I will not depart in this place. Aha! I see that you, too, Bishop, fear men more than God. I tell you that neither I nor my companion will ever depart in this place; and now, because you have yielded through human respect, the time of my dwelling in the body of this wretched creature has been prolonged."

"I care not for this prating," answered the Bishop: "thou shall depart on this very spot."

"I swear by the Sacred Blood I shall not," shrieked the demon, in a rage, tell you that, on your account, the days of my possession have been prolonged. I will depart only in that infamous house. (Here Satan made use of a vile term, to express the Church of God.) You have taken away the platform, but, by the Sacred Blood, you must put it up again. Whether you will or not, you must obey God. Accursed be this hour, in which I must tell you the truth! but I am forced to do it."

"When will Cerberus depart?" asked the Bishop.

"If you bring the wretch where I've told you," answered Satan, "he will leave next Saturday."

"And thou, when wilt thou leave?"

"Next Tuesday. But first, I want you to take all those idols out of the church—those pictures and images of yours." Satan has a horror of holy pictures and images, because he knows that they remind us of our Lord and His saints, and encourage us to imitate their virtues.

The Bishop was moved, at last, by the prayers of the Catholics, and by the entreaties of hundreds who came from distant cities, to continue the exorcism again in the Cathedral. The devil, however, protested that he would not leave unless they would resume the solemn processions which they had at first, "for such was the will of God." The Bishop and the clergy, after much hesitation, resolved, at length, to begin the processions once more.

In order to stop the mouths of the raving Calvinists, who misinterpreted and blasphemed everything sacred, Mr. Wm. Gorret, the Royal Notary, was summoned to observe and note down everything that Nicola said and did. The exorcisms took place in the presence of from ten to twelve thousand witnesses.

During the exorcism which took place on Friday, the first of February, the Bishop asked, "When will Cerberus depart?"

"I've told you before," answered Satan sullenly. "He will leave tomorrow."

"What sign will Cerberus give of his departure?"

"He will carry away a pane of glass from the window of the side-chapel."

"When wilt thou depart?"

"Next Tuesday; and I'll carry off the head of the little bailiff of Vervins. Yes, by the—I will do it, for he has given it to me." The bailiff was one of those who would not believe that Nicola was possessed. He had said several times, in a boasting tone: "Well! if that's the devil, then let him go to—and he may take my head along with him."

The abbot of St. Vincent now wrote the names of Beelzebub and Cerberus on some slips of paper, in order to burn them, and thereby torture the evil spirit.

The devil turned towards him in a fury: "He! abbot of St. Vincent!" he shrieked, "you son of a wh—e! what are you doing here? I'll make you stop that!" He then added, in a mocking tone, "Ha, my boy! you've made a mistake. You've put an 'h' instead of a 'b.'" This was really the case. The Bishop now burned the names, and Satan writhed in agony. The Bishop now held a cross close to Nicola's face, and said: "Behold, here, the image of that cross on which our Lord Jesus Christ suffered and died for us! I now command thee, in His name, to depart from the body of this creature of God."

"I will not depart!" answered the evil spirit, in a hoarse voice.

"Go forth, unclean spirit! I adjure thee, go forth!"

The demon turned away the face of his victim from the cross, and shrieked in rage: "Away with the gallows! Take it out of my sight! I will not depart. My hour is not yet come."

"Oh, accursed spirit!" said the Bishop, solemnly, "since neither prayer, nor the holy gospels, neither the exorcisms of the Church, nor the holy relics, can compel thee to depart, I will now show thee thy Lord and Master, and by His power I command thee."

"What do you mean?" shrieked Satan, gnashing his teeth. "Do you mean your white—?"

(Here the devil used a very unbecoming expression for the Blessed Sacrament.)

"How darest thou call our Blessed Lord by such a vile name?"

"Ha! ha! I've taught my Calvinists to nickname Him thus."

"Why, then, dost thou fear Him so much? Why dost thou fly in terror be fore His face?"

"Ha!" shrieked the devil, "it is that 'hoc,' that 'hoc,' that forces me to flee."

The devil here refers to the divine words of consecration by which the bread and wine are changed, in holy Mass, into the Body and Blood of our Lord Jesus Christ."

Cerberus Expelled

Next morning the keepers of Nicola went to Confession and Communion. During the procession, the devil turned towards them several times, and said in a contemptuous tone: "Faugh! you filthy papist toads! You've eaten the white—again!"

"Thou liest, Satan!" answered one of the keepers; "it is not the white—. It is the true Body of our Lord Jesus Christ, hidden under the sacramental veils."

"Well, I call him so; and there are many others among my brave Calvinists who call him so too." The devil then turned to Rev. Father Cotte, and said: "Aha! Cotte Cottelin, didn't you hear something flying about and whistling while you were saying Mass this morning? Ha! I tried hard to distract you, but I could not." This was really the case. Satan then laughed mockingly, and related the trick he had played on Dr. Carlier. "Ho! ho!" he cried; "didn't I pay the doctor for trying to poison me? As he was riding out in the country, on his way to the wedding, I hid myself in his horse's ear. When—didn't the horse rear and plunge! And how often the old doctor cried out: 'O Lord God! O Lord God!' Ho! ho! once he was pitched to the ground, and got a kick that injured his ribs a little! He had to go part of the way on foot. I then appeared to him in the shape of a lackey, told him I was a Calvinist, and urged him to kill this wretched papist Nicola. 'Oh!' said he, 'don't fear; she's got her share. She'll not trouble us much longer.' I then disappeared from him; and he was forced, in spite of himself, to ride three times around the gallows on the hill. His horse reared and trembled, and would not go any farther; so my brave doctor had to turn back. Ho! ho! he could not go to the wedding."

There were several persons present who declared that they had seen the doctor speaking to a stranger, who disappeared suddenly, and that the doctor rode three times around the gallows and then returned home.

The devil kept on talking quite loud during the holy Mass.

"Will you not stop talking?" said one of the priests.

"No!" answered Satan, impudently. "I will not."

"If you do not stop, I will give you a blow that will make you."

"Come on! Strike! strike!" said Satan; and he turned Nicola's face towards the priest.

The priest raised his hand, but, instead of striking Nicola's cheek, he made a cross upon her forehead.

The devil was angered by this unexpected action—he shook his head, and growled with rage.

The moment of consecration came, and Satan was instantly struck dumb. Nicola was now seized with the most frightful convulsions. Fifteen strong men were holding her down; and so great was the strength of the demon, that they were all draped with her aloft into the air. Nicola, her face turned away from the altar, remained suspended in space, over six feet above the platform, during the entire time of consecration. As soon as the consecration was over, she fell back heavily upon the platform.

During the exorcism which took place after Mass, the Bishop asked: "Where wert thou last night?" "I paid a visit to my Calvinists," answered Satan.

"Thou art a liar," said the Bishop.

"I've told you before," answered Satan, "that if I did not lie, I should not be a devil. But I tell you again, I visited my Calvinists, and they resolved to murder this wretched creature and all her accomplices. John Carlier and Anthony Etienne are the leaders of the plot. I know it is so. I myself was with them last night. It was I who advised them to do this."

The Bishop now held the Blessed Sacrament in his hand, and said: "O accursed spirit! arch-enemy of the ever Blessed God! I command thee, by the precious Blood of Jesus Christ here present, to depart from this poor woman! Depart, accursed, into the everlasting flames of hell!"

At these words, and especially at the sight of the Blessed Sacrament, the demon was so fearfully tormented, and the appearance of Nicola was so hideous and revolting, that the people turned away their eyes in horror. At last a heavy sigh was heard, and a cloud of black smoke issued from the mouth of Nicola. Cerberus was expelled, and, in sign of his departure, he broke and carried away a pane of glass from one of the side-chapels.

Again Nicola fell into a death-like swoon, and again she was brought to consciousness only by means of the Blessed Sacrament.

Sacrilegious Robbery

During the afternoon exorcism, the devil gave an account of a horrible sacrilege that had been perpetrated by the Calvinists. "Yes," cried he, "Nicholas and Anthony Etienne, and Nicholas Maigret, and Hubert Duchemin, my hardened Calvinists, stole a Host out of the church, and took it to Duchemin's house. There were no women present, because they could not keep it secret. There these men broke the host into three pieces, and after having boiled these pieces, they threw them to the cats and dogs, but the animals would not touch them."

"Thou liest, Satan!" said the Bishop, indignantly; "such a crime was not committed."

"Thou liest thyself, my shell-pate," answered Satan. "I know it for certain; I was present." The devil gave the Bishop the nickname "shell-pate," on account of the mitre he wore, which bore some resemblance to a section of a shell.

"Why did these Calvinists break and burn the Sacred Host?" asked the Bishop "Ho! ho!" shrieked the devil, with a fiendish laugh; if He were to appear on earth again, I and my brave Calvinists would treat Him worse than even the Jews did."

"Thou art a liar!" said the Bishop; "thou desirest only to excite the people by thy prating."

"Yes, I am a liar," answered Satan; "it was I who first invented lying. But when my master forces me, I can also tell the truth."

"Who is thy Lord and Master?"

"Do you not know Him?"

"Why dost thou accuse these men since thou hast urged them to commit this atrocious crime?"

"I do it because I am compelled," answered Satan.

Calvinist Forgery

In order to put an end to the exorcisms, the Calvinists forged two letters, written in the name of Marshal Montmorency, of Paris. These letters were addressed to the Bishop, and to the Chief Magistrate and government officials of Laon. They were written in a very bitter tone, which clearly betrayed their Calvinistic source. In these letters the Bishop and government officials were commanded to put an end to this "silly mummery" of possession and public exorcisms. The devil afterwards revealed the names of those who had forged these letters. There is, besides, clear and certain proof that Marshal Montmorency had nothing to do with them.

The good Bishop was deceived by these letters. In order to satisfy the Calvinists, he gave orders that the public processions should cease, and that the exorcisms should be carried on as privately as possible.

The next day, during the exorcism, the Bishop asked of Satan: "When wilt thou depart?"

"I shall not depart today," answered the demon, with a defiant look; "on the contrary, my days have been prolonged on your account. Ah, my shell-pate! you are too credulous. You wish to please men rather than God. Know, then, that I have now gained a respite of two days longer. I shall not depart today."

"Why so?" asked the Bishop, in astonishment.

"Ha! you gave credit to letters that were forged by my brave Calvinists. It was I who tempted you to do this." (To give credit to the letters.)

"Silence, thou lying spirit!" said the Bishop, indignantly. "I will soon expel thee by the power of the precious Blood of Jesus Christ."

"By whom?" asked the devil, in a rage; "by your white—?"

"Cease thy blasphemies, accursed spirit!" cried the Bishop. "He is thy Lord. His very presence puts thee to flight."

"Ah! yes, yes!" howled the demon, wildly; "it is true. It is that 'hoc,' that 'hoc,' that forces me to flee."

Next day, during the exorcism, Satan gave the names of the Calvinists who had forged these letters: they were Mr. Bayard, Anthony and Nicholas Etienne, and Dr. Carlier. He related many other circumstances, which were found to be perfectly true.

The name of Beelzebub was then burned by the Bishop in the flames of a blessed candle. This caused the demon the most fearful torments. He reared like a wild ox, he writhed like a wounded serpent, he gnashed his teeth, and shrieked: "Oh! you hound of a bishop! I'll pay you for that!"

"Begone, Satan!" answered the Bishop; "I fear thee not."

The Bishop now began to read the holy gospels, and the solemn words of the exorcism. Satan instantly began to mimic his tone and gestures. He put on a comic air of piety, bowed the head, mumbled some prayers, and repeated the words of the Bishop with comic gravity. When the Bishop said, "Ergo, maledicte diabole, da honorem Deo vivo," Satan answered: "No! I will honor none but myself. Do you honor Him, if you choose."

At the words, "Maledicte diabole, damnate atque damnande," Satan said: "Why do you repeat these words so often? I know already that I am damned!"

At the words, "Recognosce sententiam tuam," Satan answered: "Do not trouble yourself, I know my sentence already."

The Bishop once made a slight mistake in reading an exorcism, and Satan corrected him instantly. "Ah, my shell-pate!" cried he, in a mocking tone, "you've made a mistake; it is not 'magister daemonum,' but 'daemonum magister.' Look a little closer—put on your spectacles."

At the words, "Dux furum, bonorum, insidiator," and the like, the demon clapped his hands and burst forth into a wild satanic laugh, that made the church walls ring again. "Ha! ha!" he screamed, "what pleasure you give me! Ho! repeat those words. Ha! they are my titles of honor."

The Bishop then held the Blessed Sacrament in his hand, and expelled Satan once more by means of our Lord's Sacred Body.

In the afternoon of the fifth of February, the usual procession was begun. As the devil saw the procession forming, he began to ridicule the clergy.

"He! he!" cried he, in mockery; "what are you doing? making a procession in the afternoon?"

During the first round of the procession, Satan whistled and sang, and mimicked the choir-boys who sang the Litany. During the second round of the procession, Satan became a little quieter. Very soon he began to gnash his teeth, and spit in the faces of those around him. He writhed, and shrieked in a rage to the mayor, who carried the cross, "Ha, mayor! turn back! that's a good fellow; don't go any farther!" But the mayor would not heed him, and continued his way leisurely.

During the third round of the procession, the demon shrieked: "Oh, mayor! abominable mayor! turn back! Ah! you miserable wretch! you will make me furious. Will you turn back? A thousand million devils, and children of the devils, take you, mayor, and your wife!"

He also called out to the choir-boys, who accompanied the Blessed Sacrament with lighted tapers, "Ha, you bastards! blow out those candles! You will make me wild!"

During the exorcism the Bishop said to Satan: "Tell me, when wilt thou depart?"

"Next Thursday afternoon, at three o'clock. But I will not leave the city, you understand. I will go to Mr. Carlier."

"Thou shalt not go to Mr. Carlier."

"Thou liest!" shrieked the demon; "Carlier and all the Calvinists are mine. I repeat it again. If Jesus Christ were yet on earth, I and my Calvinists would treat Him worse than the Jews did."

"Why dost thou speak so bitterly of the Calvinists?" asked the Bishop.

"Because they are hardened in sin, and I will make them still more hardened."

The Bishop burned the name of Beelzebub once more. At this Satan shrieked in a rage: "May the thunderbolt strike thee, dog of a Bishop!"

It is worthy of notice that Satan became more furious as the hour of his departure drew nearer.

During the exorcism which took place the next morning, the sixth of February, the Bishop said to Satan, "Where wilt thou go when expelled from the body of this creature of God?"

"I will go to St. Nicholas Du-Bois, to enter the body of a woman, for the possession of whom two devils are already quarreling; for, when we are driven out of one person, we go to take possession of someone else."

"Who are those two devils?"

"They are Cerberus, and a little devil poor wretch! a puppy who has no name."

"To which rank does he belong?"

"To that of Cerberus."

"Are there, then, a great many devils?"

"Yes! more than there are flakes of snow in a heavy snow-storm."

At these words, a murmur of astonishment was heard throughout the church.

"Oh, accursed spirit!" said the Bishop, "I command thee, in the name of the Holy Trinity, to leave the body of this woman, and to depart to the flames of hell."

"No, I will not!" answered the demon; "it is not yet time. I must first do more mischief."

"Thou shalt not!" replied the Bishop; "I will expel thee instantly."

"Ah, yes! I know that I must depart, but not today. Before I leave I must get back the piece of money which I gave to the little monk of Vervins, and I swear, by the Sacred Blood, I will not leave until I get it."

(The little monk of whom Satan here spoke, was de Motta. During the exorcism which took place at Vervins, Satan had given him a piece of money. No one knew where the evil spirit got this money. On giving it to de Motta, he said, "Here, my little preacher, keep this money. I must get it back when I am leaving this body.")

A messenger was instantly sent to de Motta, who was then at Velly, for the piece of money. Satan, seeing the messenger depart, screamed after him: "He! you bastard! I see you. By the—, if you go to Velly, I will send you home in a hurry!"

The priest encouraged the messenger, and hung around his neck a golden cross which was filled with relics. No harm befell the good man on his journey, as he was protected by the precious relics, and by the holy angels, to whom he continually recommended himself. Satan was again expelled by means of the Blessed Sacrament.

During the evening, as Nicola was undisturbed by the evil spirit, the priest advised her to make her confession. After she had finished her confession, the priest was about to give her absolution, when suddenly the devil took possession of her, and sprang upon the priest, struck and kicked him, and screamed, in a rage: "Ha, ha! do you think you are more cunning than I am? I saw you; you wanted to give her absolution, but I will not allow it. Go about your business, now!"

The bystanders were filled with terror on seeing the great power of Satan. What fearful harm would he not do, if God would not restrain him?

During the exorcism which took place on the morning of the seventh of February, the Bishop asked Satan once more: "When wilt thou depart?"

"Very soon," answered Satan; "this very evening, at the same hour in which I took possession of this wretch. Oh, my shell-pate! my shell-pate! I tempted you to get angry at your servant. I watched you yesterday, and the days previous. You took no supper. But this is not yet all. I will do you more harm before I leave this place."

During the exorcism, the devil suddenly looked around, and said: "He, he! stop! stop! There is a sorcerer in the church, and some pickpockets." He then looked fixedly in a certain direction, and said, at last, "Tis done—the pocket is picked." He then spat in the face of Mr. Gorret, the Royal Notary, and said: "You've had enough to do these last few days, Mr. Notary! Is it not so?"

The Bishop then said to Satan: "What sign wilt thou give of thy departure?"

"I will cure Nicola's left arm, so that she can use it as well as ever. Is not this a splendid miracle? You will find another sign on the roof of the belfry."

"What hast thou gained by taking possession of this body?" asked the Bishop. "Many have been converted by witnessing the great power of the Blessed Sacrament. Depart, then! everyone hates and despises thee."

"I know it," answered Satan. "Many have been converted; but there are also many who remain hardened in their sins."

"Tell me, then, why hast thou taken possession of this honest and virtuous Catholic woman?"

"I have done so by permission of God. I have taken possession of her on account of the sins of the people. I have done it to show my Calvinists that there are devils who can take possession of men whenever God permits it. I know they do not want to believe this; but I will show them that I am a devil. I have taken possession of this creature in order to convert them, or to harden them in their sins; and, by the Sacred Blood, I shall perform my task."

This answer filled all who heard it with horror. "Yes," answered the Bishop, solemnly, "God desires to unite all men in the one holy faith. As there is but one God, so there can be but one true religion. A religion like that which the Protestants have invented, is but a hollow mockery. It must fall. The religion established by our Lord Jesus Christ is the only true one, which shall last forever; it shall increase. It is destined to unite all men within its sacred embrace, so that there shall be but one sheepfold and one Shepherd. This Divine Shepherd is our Lord Jesus Christ, the invisible Head of the holy Roman Catholic Church, whose visible Head is our holy Father the Pope, successor of St. Peter."

The devil was silent—he was put to shame before the entire multitude. He was expelled, once more, by means of the Blessed Sacrament.

In the afternoon of the same day, the devil began to prate and make merry during the procession. "Ah! ha!" cried he: "you're mistaken, this time. Do you think you can expel me, after having taken your dinner? I forgot to tell you, my shell-pate, that you should have fasted today. Had you done so, I should have been obliged to leave today. Now I have gained one day more. Hu, hu! ha, ha! he, he! I have gained another day! I am more cunning than you, my shell-pate. You do not understand the Scriptures." Satan here refers to the words of our Lord in the gospels: that there are some devils who can be expelled only by prayer and fasting. The devil then laughed, sang, and whistled, in the greatest glee.

As soon as the procession was ended, the exorcism began as usual.

"Now thou shall depart at last," said the Bishop.

"Ah, yes! I would have done so, had you not taken your dinner. He! tell me: don't you know that you cannot expel a prince of devils like myself, after you have eaten and drunk your fill?"

"I have not eaten so much that I cannot expel thee," said the Bishop.

"Oh yes, yes! you have eaten much! I saw you, and those who were at table with you." The devil here mentioned the names of the Bishop's guests.

"Thou shalt not deceive me by thy prating," said the Bishop; "thou art a liar! I will soon expel thee."

"Yes, I am a liar. But I shall not depart, for you have not been to confession."

"Thou liest!" said the Bishop, indignantly; "I have been to confession."

(We may remark here, that the Bishop and clergy went to confession every morning before beginning the exorcism. Experience shows that the purer and more free from sin one is, the more terrible is he to Satan.)

"You have confessed," said the devil, "but what kind of confession was it? You accused yourself only in a general way. You only said that you were angry with your servant and with the chaplain. Had you told this sin, and this," said the demon, mentioning certain faults, "I should not know anything of them, and I could not reproach you as I do now."

At these Words of Satan, a loud murmur of astonishment was heard throughout the church.

"Ha!" said the devil; "you think that you can expel me in this way? You have not the proper attendance of a Bishop. Where are the Dean and the Archdean? Where are the Royal Judges? Where is the Chief Magistrate, who was frightened out of his wits at night, in the prison? Where is the Procurator of the King? Where are his Attorneys and Counsellors? Where is the Clerk of the Court?" (The devil mentioned each of these by name.) "I will not depart until all are assembled. Were I to depart now, what proof could you give to the king of all that has happened? Do you think that people will believe you so easily? No! no! There are many who would make objections. The testimony of these common country-people here will have but little weight. It is a torment to me that I must tell you what you have to do. I am forced to do it. Ha! cursed be the hour in which I first took possession of this vile wretch!"

"I find little pleasure in thy prating," answered the Bishop; "there are witnesses enough here. Those whom you have mentioned are not necessary. Depart, then! give glory to God. Depart—go to the flames of hell!"

"Yes, I shall depart, but not today. I know full well that I must depart. My sentence is passed; I am compelled to leave; but, before I do so, you must fast a little more. You are not lean enough yet."

"I care not for thy jabbering," said the Bishop, "I shall expel thee by the power of God; by the precious Blood of our Lord Jesus Christ."

"Yes, I must yield to you," shrieked the demon, wildly. "It tortures me that I must give you this honor.

It is now twelve hundred years since a Bishop like you expelled the prince of devils."

"Thou art a liar!" said the Bishop, solemnly. "Every day the holy Roman Catholic Church triumphs over thee and thy hellish spirits."

"Thou liest thyself, my shell-pate!" answered Satan. "Poor, contemptible devils, nameless wretches, may have been expelled, but the prince of devils has not been expelled."

The Bishop now burned the name of Beelzebub, but Satan only laughed at him, and said: "Oh, my shell-pate, you are burning only paper and ink!"

At this everyone was astonished, as the burning of the demon's name had hitherto always caused him the most frightful tortures.

"I see," said the Bishop, "that thou heedest neither the exorcisms nor the burning of thy name; I will, therefore, show thee thy Lord and Master."

"Whom do you mean?" shrieked the demon, in a fury. "Do you mean your white—?"

Satan was at length expelled. On leaving, he cried out: "I depart, but I shall return again. My hour is not yet come."

The next day, as Nicola was being taken to the church, the demon instantly took possession of her."

"Aha!" cried he, in a mocking tone, "I am not gone away yet." Then he ridiculed all that had been done the day previous. During the exorcism, the Bishop said: "Why dost thou not depart? The appointed day and hour has come."

"I will not go, because you are not fasting, because you have not been to confession, because you have not assembled witnesses enough."

The Bishop now took the Blessed Sacrament in his hand, and held it close to the face of the possessed woman.

"A thousand million devils take you, wretched shell-pate! Why do you torture me so horribly?"

At last, Satan was compelled to flee once more.

The next morning, after the procession was ended, the Holy Sacrifice of the Mass was offered up, as usual. As soon as the possessed woman was brought upon the platform, the devil looked around the church and said: "Ha! there are only papists here! The assembly is not yet full. Where is the magistrate Du Manche, who was in such mortal terror, at night, in the prison? Where is Bochet, the State's attorney? Where is the Archdean? I shall not leave until all are present; for, by the Sacred Blood, I have good reasons for it."

During holy Mass, a German Protestant, named Stephen Voske, happened to be in church. Hearing his name called by the demon, he went up to the platform to speak to him. Voske spoke in German, but the demon answered him in French.

"Ha! you want me to speak German with you; but I will not do it. Were I in your country, I would speak German better than you do. I can easily see that you were not brought up in Germany." (This was really the case.) "Here," said Satan, "I speak only the language of the country, so that everyone can understand me. You may speak German; I will answer you in my own language."

They continued thus to talk together for about half an hour, one speaking German, and the other French. When the time for the consecration approached, Satan said to Voske: "Stop, now! keep silence! They are going to show the white—. Ha! it is my white—. It is I who have nicknamed Him thus. I have taught all my servants and disciples to do the same."

Suddenly, Satan was struck dumb. The possessed woman is raised over six feet into the air, and then falls back heavily upon the platform. The same scene is repeated at the Elevation of the Chalice. The demon, wild with rage, shrieked: "Ha! Bishop, you shell-pate!

if I had you now I would make you suffer for this. You torture me horribly."

(We must remark here, that the Bishop purposely prolonged the time of consecration, in order to cause Satan greater torment.)

As the Bishop, just before the Pater Noster, took the Sacred Host once more in his hand, and raised it with the chalice, the possessed woman was again whisked into the air, carrying with her the keepers, fifteen in number, at least six feet above the platform; and, after awhile, she fell heavily back to the ground.

At this sight, all present were filled with amazement and terror. The German Protestant fell on his knees: he burst into tears; he was converted.

"Ah!" cried he, "I now believe firmly that the devil really possesses this poor creature. I believe that it is really the Body and Blood of Jesus Christ which expels him. I believe firmly. I will no longer remain a Protestant."

After Mass, the exorcism began as usual. As soon as the Bishop appeared on the platform, Satan cried, in a mocking tone: "Ah, ha! my shell-pate! you made a good confession this morning to the dean. I saw you, but I could not understand your words."

"Now, at last," said the Bishop, "thou must depart. Away with thee, evil spirit!"

"Yes," said Satan, "it is true that I must depart, but not yet. I shall not go before the hour is come in which I first took possession of this wretched creature. Have patience, then; wait until three o'clock. Oh, accursed be that hour! Do not push on the clock. I know the hour well. My sentence is already passed."

"What sign wilt thou give of thy departure?" asked the Bishop.

"Never mind!" answered Satan, sullenly; "you shall have signs enough. I shall heal the left arm of this creature. She has not been able to use it these three months, because I possessed it. And you, my shell-pate! you shall have your sign. I shall strike such a terror to your heart as you never felt before, and which you will not soon forget."

"Where wert thou last night?"

"I was in your palace," answered Satan. "I saw you right well. You got up last night to pray. It was about three o'clock. I know that your prayers have helped much to expel me."

Satan then turned to a gentleman present named Lancelot May, and publicly accused his brother Robert of some very grievous sins, which he named.

"Yes," cried Satan, in a rage, "I swear by the Sacred Blood that what I say is true, even though he is your brother."

He then turned to a woman, who stood near by, and said: "He! Margaret, your husband, Lancelot, lost two dollars last night. It is Nelly who won them."

At this, Lancelot, who was himself present, hung his head in shame, and all present were greatly surprised. He continued, for some time, to reveal thus the sins of those around him. At last the Bishop took the Sacred Host in his hand, and said: "In the name of the Adorable Trinity, Father, Son, and Holy Ghost—in the name of the Sacred Body of Jesus Christ here present I command thee, wicked spirit, to depart."

"What!" shrieked Satan, "you wish to expel me with your white—?"

"Accursed spirit!" said the Bishop, indignantly; "who has taught thee to blaspheme God thus?"

"It was I who taught it to my Calvinists, who are my obedient servants," answered Satan.

"But it is the Sacred Body of thy Lord and Master; it is the Blessed Body of our Lord Jesus Christ. By His power thou shalt be expelled."

"Yes, yes, it is true!" shrieked the demon, wildly; "it is true. It is the Body of God. I must confess it, for

I am forced to do so. Ha! it tortures me that I must confess this; but I must. I speak the truth only when I am forced to do it. The truth is not from me. It comes from my Lord and Master. I have entered this body by the permission of God."

The Bishop now held the Blessed Sacrament close to the face of the possessed woman. The demon writhed in fearful agony. He tried in every way to escape from the presence of our Lord in the Blessed Sacrament.

At length a black smoke was seen issuing from the mouth of Nicola. She fell into a swoon, and was restored again to consciousness only by means of the Blessed Sacrament.

Last Exorcism

8th of February.—During the procession, which took place in the afternoon of the same day, the devil said to the Bishop: "Oh Bishop, my shell-pate! you have taken no dinner. You are sick and weary," And then he began to sing—"Oh, he has eaten nothing! I knew that you had to fast before you could drive me out of the body of this worthless wretch."

After the procession, Nicola was again placed on the platform, where she was held by fifteen strong men.

The Bishop and clergy then offered up a solemn prayer in Latin, in which they called the devil a spirit accursed.

"Why do you use that word accursed?" asked the devil, angrily.

"Because," answered the Bishop, "thou hast offended God so grievously, that thou canst never hope for pardon. Thou art lost to all love and hope; thou hast nought but eternal damnation to expect. Thy sentence is passed forever."

At these words Satan became silent, and turned away.

The Bishop now began the last solemn adjuration. During the exorcism, the devil said several times to the Bishop: "Ah, you have taken no dinner today! You are very weak." He then looked around, and said: "Ha, ha! are you here, Attorney-General Bochet? You were not here this morning!"

He then blew out the blessed candle which stood near the Bishop, and said, with a mocking laugh, "Ha, ha! how stupid you are to burn candles in the broad day light!"

The Bishop read the gospels, prayers and exorcisms; he burned Beelzebub's name, showed him the relic of the holy cross, and solemnly commanded him to depart.

The devil answered impudently, that he did not feel like going yet.

"I shall not ask thee any longer," said the Bishop, "when thou intendest to leave; I shall expel thee instantly by the power of the living God, and by the precious Body and Blood of Jesus Christ, His beloved Son, here present in the Sacrament of the Altar."

"Ha, yes!" shrieked the demon; "I confess that the Son of God is here really and truly present. He is my Lord and Master. It tortures me to confess it, but I am forced to do so." Then he repeated several times, with a wild, unearthly howl: " Yes, it is true. I must confess it. I am forced to leave, by the power of God's Body here present. I must—I must depart. It torments me that I must go so soon, and that I must confess this truth. But this truth is not from me; it comes from my Lord and Master, who has sent me hither, and who commands and compels me to confess the truth publicly. I shall go, but I shall not go empty-handed. By the Sacred Blood, I shall have my booty. I shall take along with me the head of the little bailiff of Vervius. Perhaps I could also take with me some of my Calvinists—body and soul—for they belong to me. He! give me your head!" cried he, turning to the Bishop; "let me see whether I cannot carry it off?"

"No, never!" answered the Bishop; "thou shalt depart, and thou shalt take nothing with thee. These men are baptized—thou canst not touch them."

"Yes," cried Satan, in a mocking tone, "they are baptized; but, after having renounced me in baptism, they gave themselves up to me again. Therefore they are mine—they are surely mine!"

"I forbid thee, in the name of the living God," said the Bishop, "to hurt either them or anyone here present."

The Bishop then took the Blessed Sacrament in his hand, and, holding It on high, he said, with a solemn voice: "O thou wicked, unclean spirit, Beelzebub! thou arch-enemy of the eternal God! behold, here present, the precious Body and Blood of our Lord Jesus Christ, thy Lord and Master! I adjure thee, in the name and by the power of our Lord and Saviour Jesus Christ, true God and true man, Who is here present; I command thee to depart instantly and forever, from this creature of God. Depart to the deepest depth of hell, there to be tormented forever. Go forth, unclean spirit, go forth—behold here thy Lord and Master!"

At these solemn words, and at the sight of our Sacramental Lord, the poor possessed woman writhed fearfully. Her limbs cracked as if every bone in her body were breaking. The fifteen strong men who held her, could scarcely keep her back. They staggered from side to side, they were covered with perspiration. Satan tried to escape from the presence of our Lord in the Blessed Sacrament. The mouth of Nicola was wide open, her tongue hung down below her chin, her face was shockingly swollen and distorted. Her color changed from yellow to green, and became even gray and blue, so that she no longer looked like a human being; it was rather the face of a hideous, incarnate demon. All present trembled with terror, especially when they heard the wild cry of the demon, which sounded like the loud roar of a wild bull.

They fell on their knees, and, with tears in their eyes, began to cry out: "Jesus, have mercy!"

The Bishop continued to urge Satan. At last the evil spirit departed, and Nicola fell back senseless into the arms of her keepers. She still, however, remained shockingly distorted. In this state she was shown to the judges, and to all the people present; she was rolled up like a ball. The Bishop now fell on his knees, in order to give her the Blessed Sacrament as usual. But see! suddenly the demon returns, wild with rage, endeavors to seize the hand of the Bishop, and tries even to grasp the Blessed Sacrament Itself. The Bishop starts back—Nicola is carried into the air, and the Bishop rises from his knees, trembling with terror and pale as death.

The good Bishop takes courage again: he pursues the demon, holding the Blessed Sacrament in his hand. Satan endeavors to escape, and hurls the keepers to the ground.

The people call upon God for aid.

Satan departs once more, with a noise which resembles a crash of thunder.

Suddenly he returns again in a fury, and casts a look of rage on some Calvinists present, who stood the whole time with covered heads.

"On your knees!" cried the people; "uncover your heads; kneel down in the presence of the precious Body and Blood of our Lord Jesus Christ."

Scarcely had these words been uttered, when a wild cry was heard, "To arms! to arms!" In an instant all was in confusion.

The Catholics thought that the Calvinists had come armed to church, in order to massacre them. The Calvinists, on the other hand, were filled with mortal terror. Soon this fear and confusion spread throughout the city. Every one was terrified, but no one could tell the real cause of such a sudden uproar.

The Bishop remained calmly at his post. Still holding the Blessed Sacrament in his hand, he turned towards the people, and said, in a loud voice, "My friends, do not be disturbed. Remain where you are. Here is the true Body of our Lord Jesus Christ; He will assist us; on your knees, and pray to God. I beg you, in the name of God, do not hurt one another."

Scarcely had the Bishop uttered these words, when all was instantly calm again. The people fell on their knees, and prayed to God for the possessed woman. The Bishop still pursued and urged Satan, holding the Blessed Sacrament in his hand, till at length the demon, overcome by the power of our Lord's Sacred Body, went forth amidst smoke, and lightning, and thunder.

Thus was the demon at length expelled forever, on Friday afternoon, at three o'clock, the same day and hour on which our Lord triumphed over hell by His ever-blessed death.

Nicola was now completely cured; she could move her left arm with the greatest ease. She now fell on her knees, and thanked God, and the good Bishop, for all he had done for her.

The people wept for joy, and sang hymns of praise and thanksgiving in honor of God, and of our dear Lord in the Blessed Sacrament.

On all sides were heard the exclamations: "Oh, what a great miracle! Oh, thank God that I witnessed it! Who is there now that could doubt of the Real Presence of our Lord Jesus Christ in the Sacrament of the Altar!"

Many Protestants present also said: "I believe now in the Presence of our Lord in the Blessed Sacrament; I have seen it with my eyes! I will remain a Calvinist no longer. Accursed be those who have hitherto kept me in error! Oh, now I can understand what a good thing is the Holy Sacrifice of the Mass!"

A solemn Te Deum was intoned; the organ pealed forth, and the bells rung a merry chime. The whole city was filled with joy.

Chapter III

Spiritualism, or (Better) Spiritism

It is now over twenty years (1847) since the notorious Fox girls began to attract public attention by their spirit-rappings. At first, the spirits communicated by rapping and moving furniture; but now, besides rapping mediums, there are writing mediums, seeing and speaking mediums! Modern science is altogether unable to account for, or to disprove, the alleged facts of spiritualism; but this is because modern science, or rather what passes for science, refuses to acknowledge the existence of the superhuman and supernatural. To deny the reality of all the alleged spirit manifestations, is to discredit all human testimony; and to regard them all as jugglery, as the result of trickery, is equally absurd. No one, who reflects a little, will pretend to say that so many thousands and even millions of spiritualists—among whom are numbers of men and women noted for their intelligence and honesty—no one, I say, will pretend that all these are only playing tricks upon one another. Tell me, in the name of sound reason, what object could all these fathers and mothers, brothers and sisters, friends and relatives, have in thus deceiving one another, and pretending to have communications from spirits, if they really have none? Those who can swallow such an absurdity, are certainly far more weak-minded and credulous than those who believe in the reality of spirit manifestations.

It is certain that there is often a great deal of jugglery and trickery in these so-called spirit manifestations. It is also certain that there is much which can be explained on natural principles. There is much which proceeds from the morbid or abnormal affections of human nature, from imagination or hallucination; but, admitting all this, there still remains a great deal that can be explained only by admitting the interference of superhuman and intelligent powers. Some try to explain the phenomena of spiritualism by attributing them all to animal magnetism, or to a force which they call "od," or "odyllic," force. But what "odyllic " force means, they are unable to say; and so, with this newly-coined word, they only seek to cover their ignorance.

Spiritualists pretend that these phenomena are produced by departed spirits, but of this they have no other proof than the assertion of the spirits themselves. Now, according to the testimony of all Spiritualists, many, I might say all, of these spirits are liars, and consequently their assertions cannot be credited. The truth is, we cannot conclude anything certain from these phenomena without the aid of revelation. I do not pretend to say that all science is necessarily based on faith, but I do say that, without the light of revelation, we cannot have a full knowledge of the various phenomena of the universe, or explain the various facts of history. If I did not know, from revelation, that the devil and his angels exist, I might observe, and be convinced of, the various manifestations of spiritualism, and yet I could not trace them with certainty to their true source; they would remain to me inexplicable. But, knowing from revelation that even the very air swarms with evil spirits—the enemies of God and man—I can see at once the natural explanation of the spirit manifestations, and trace them to their proper source. This source is none other than hell. With Father Bonaventure, I boldly assert that "modern spiritualism is nothing but Satanism." The proofs for the truth of this assertion, I take—

From the holiness of God and His angels.

From the answers of the spirits themselves.

From the character of these spirit-manifestations and visitations.

From the behavior of the spirits when in the presence of some supernatural power.

From the principles and morals of the spiritualists.

From the baneful consequences of spiritualism.

From Holy Scripture and the Church.

I

As to the origin of these spirit-manifestations, I say they cannot come from God, or His holy angels or saints. God and His angels and saints are too holy and too sublime beings to amuse vain men with such frivolous entertainments. Good and holy spirits hate what God hates; they will never do anything that is an abomination in the sight of God. The spirit-manifestations must, then, proceed from evil spirits, from Satan and his associates.

II

The answers of these spirits are such that they betray, at once, their author. "Out of thy own mouth I judge thee, O wicked servant!" (Luke xix. 22.) The Spiritualists themselves assert that the spirits from whom they receive communications, often speak ambiguously; that they do not always tell the truth, but that, in many instances, they have told palpable lies. Now does not this betray their satanic character? To tell a lie is a sin. But holy spirits cannot sin anymore. These lying spirits, then, are evil spirits. Satan is a liar, and the father of lies. He is the inveterate enemy of truth, and, if he sometimes tells it, it is because he is compelled by a higher power; or if, now and then, of his own accord, it is only because truth serves his purpose of deception better than falsehood.

The predictions of God are clear and precise, for, with God, the future is ever present. But Satan is a creature, and his power and intelligence, though superhuman, are yet limited. The universe has many secrets which he cannot penetrate. The devil can never tell the future with certainty; he can only guess at it, like a shrewd observer, judging from his knowledge of the present and the past. Hence it is that the oracles of

Satan are always ambiguous and stammering, and calculated to deceive; in most instances, they turn out to be falsehoods. Now the holy, good spirits never speak ambiguously, or in a manner calculated to deceive; they never tell lies, for they can sin no more. It is, then, evident that those lying spirits, with whom Spiritualists communicate, must be evil spirits.

III

The visitations or communications of God, or of His angels, bring peace and holy joy; while the communications or visitations of the devil, on the contrary, bring trouble and discord.

When the Lord comes in His gracious visitations, all is sweetness and peace. No disturbance of the physical system, no whirling and howling, no storm and tempest, no wringing and twisting of the arms and legs, no violent and indecent postures, no abnormal development or exercise of the faculties, mark the incoming of the Holy Ghost. All is calm and serene. The understanding is illuminated, the heart is warmed, the will is strengthened, and the whole soul is elevated by the infusion of a supernatural grace. There is no crisis, no forgetfulness, or awaking from a trance.

But whenever it is the reverse, as is the case in spiritism—whenever there is violence, distortion, quaking, trembling, and disturbance—there are so many indications of the presence of the evil spirit, which delights in violence and disorder, and which displays power without love, force without goodness, knowledge without gentleness.

Besides, it is a well-attested fact, that many of the so-called spirit-mediums understand Greek, Latin, Spanish, and French, when they have no knowledge of any language but their own; and that often there has been speaking and writing in foreign languages and unknown tongues by those who were unacquainted with either. Some of them see and tell things passing in distant places, and exhibit a superior physical strength.

A daughter of Judge Edmonds, a celebrated Spiritualist, when about eight or ten years old, wrote, in a trance, Arabic, Hebrew, and Latin. Mr. Hume, in England, some time ago, carried fire in his hands, lengthened his arms, flew up in the air, and was shining bright sometimes.

Facts like these evidently betray a diabolical agent, and even satanic possession; for they are precisely the same as those laid down by the Catholic Church for the guidance of exorcists in cases of supposed demoniac invasion or possession.

IV

The good angels do all in their power to promote the kingdom of Jesus Christ on earth. They remind us of the gospel-truths, and encourage us to live up to them: whilst those spirits with whom Spiritualists hold intercourse, make most strenuous efforts to destroy Christianity. Jesus Christ triumphed over the devil by His death on the cross; He broke his power. Hence it is that Satan bears an implacable hatred to Jesus Christ and His religion.

What wonder, then, if we find that he is always engaged in undermining Christianity, and destroying all belief in it?

The doctrines which these spirits teach, and confirm with lying wonders, are evidently what St. Paul calls "the doctrines of the devils." These lying spirits all unite in denying the existence of hell and of devils. They also deny the resurrection of the body; they give a false idea of God; they assert that Christianity has had its day, and that they have come to announce a new and more sublime form of religion—a religion which shall free the world from the Old Church, from bondage to the Bible, from creeds and dogmas—a religion which shall free mankind from the laws of social and political life, and shall place the religious and political world on a higher basis, and infuse into it a more energetic spirit of progress. Such is the high-sounding boast of spiritualism and its infernal agents. In the eyes of its deluded followers, spiritualism is destined to carry on and complete the work which was begun by Jesus Christ, and which, as they blasphemously assert, was left unfinished. The morals and principles taught by these lying spirits are as bad as can be imagined; and, in fact, the lives led by some of the more advanced Spiritualists are most immoral and revolting. The spirits, it is true, give, now and then, some good advice: they sometimes tell the truth; for, as the Apostle assures us, the devil sometimes "puts on the semblance of an angel of light." But he does this only to gain credit, and to secure the confidence of his deluded followers. He sometimes tells the truth, but it is always blended with or followed by falsehood. He sometimes gives good advice, but, at the same time, he takes away all moral restraints. The evil spirit may sometimes advise persons to become Catholics, but it is only that they may receive the sacraments unworthily, and thus become hardened in sin, and incapable of returning to the truth, and that thus he may acquire more power over them. After some time, he always advises them to leave the Catholic Church. We have numerous instances of this.

Dr. Nichols, from Philadelphia, and Mr. Hume, were told by the devil to become Catholics; and, after some time, the devil said to them, "Now leave the Catholic Church, and ascend higher."

These lying spirits war against all authority in faith and morals, as being repugnant to the rights of reason; they war against all authority in social and domestic life, as being repugnant to the sentiments of the heart. They assert that all should seek and do what is right, but that no one should be constrained. The affections and passions should be free as the air we breathe, and to restrain them, say these lying spirits, is to war against nature herself. These hellish spirits often speak to their deluded followers of love, but the love which they preach is not the love of God. No! it is only sexual love; base, animal passion! Hence the spiritualists very generally look upon the marriage law as tyrannical and absurd, and assert the doctrine of free love. They hold that sexual love is the essence of marriage, and that, when that love ceases, the marriage is dissolved.

They, therefore, consider it immoral for a husband and wife to live together, after they have ceased to love each other. It is easy to see to what such a doctrine leads, and we are not at all surprised to find that conjugal fidelity is not considered a virtue by the greater part of Spiritualists. The Spiritualist husband may leave his wife, and the Spiritualist wife may leave her husband, and choose a new "affinity" as often as they please. At the Spiritualist Convention, held some years ago (June, 1858) at Rutland, Vt., the following resolution was presented and defended:

"Resolved, That the only true and natural marriage is an exclusive conjugal love between one man and one woman."

According to this theory, the essence of marriage is "exclusive conjugal love." Consequently, the bond of marriage is dissolved as soon as this conjugal love ceases, and a man or woman may marry as often as his or her conjugal love becomes "exclusive" for any particular individual.

A similar resolution was presented at the National Spiritualist Convention, held in Chicago, August 9, 1864. It was offered by Dr. A. G. Parker of Boston, Chairman of Committee on Social Relations.

At this famous Rutland Convention, a certain Miss Julia Branch, of New York, said, as reported in the "Banner of Light," July 10, 1858, that she must demand her freedom; she must demand her right to receive equal wages with man in payment for her labor, and her right to have children when she will and by whom she will.

We might quote much more, still more startling; we might give an account of the Spiritualist community at Berlin, Ohio, but we do not wish to disgust our respected readers. What we have said concerning the doctrines and morals of Spiritualists, is enough to prove to all that spiritualism is of satanic origin. "By their fruits you shall know them."

V

Let us see now how these familiar spirits of the Spiritualists behave when in presence of an opposing power. Such an opposing power, for instance, is a simple prayer from a Catholic priest, or even from a good Catholic layman.

St. Luke relates, in the Acts of the Apostles (chap. viii.), that a certain man, named Simon the Magician, had acquired a great reputation in the city of Samaria.

This man seduced the people by his magical practices. He gave out that he was some great one. All gave ear to him, from the least to the greatest, saying: "This man is the power of God, which is called great."

The infernal spirit tried to oppose these illusions and artifices to the true miracles of Christ, as he was suffered to assist the magicians of the King Pharaoh against Moses. But God, when He permits the devil to exert in so extraordinary a manner his natural strength and powers, always furnishes His servants with the means of discerning and confounding the imposture.

Accordingly, the clear miracles wrought, at that time, by St. Philip the Deacon, put the magician quite out of countenance. Being himself witness to them, and seeing the people run to Philip, he also believed, or rather pretended to believe, and, being baptized, he stuck close to Philip, hoping to attain to the power of effecting miracles like those which he saw him perform. The Apostles of Jerusalem, learning of the conversion of Samaria, sent thither St. Peter and St. John to confirm the converts by the imposition of hands. With the grace of the Sacrament of Confirmation, at that time, were usually conferred certain external gifts of the miraculous powers. Simon, seeing these communicated to the laity by the imposition of the hands of the

Apostles, offered them money, saying, "Give me also this power, that on whomsoever I shall lay my hands he may receive the Holy Ghost." But St. Peter said to him: "Keep thy money to thyself, to perish with thee, because thou hast thought that the gift of God may be purchased with money. Do penance for this thy wickedness, and pray to God, if perhaps this thought of thy heart may be forgiven thee. For I see thou art in the gall of bitterness, and engaged in the bonds of iniquity."

Simon, fearing the threat of temporal evils, answered: "Pray you for me to the Lord that none of these things may come upon me."

The Fathers of the Church generally look upon the conversion of Simon to the faith as an act of hypocrisy, founded only in ambition and temporal views, and in the hope of purchasing the gifts of the Holy Ghost, which he ascribed to a superior magical art.

Simon the Magician, having then been confounded in Samaria, went to Rome, where he gained a high reputation. St. Justin Martyr, St. Iræneus, Tertullian, Eusebius, and others, assure us that divine honors were paid to him there. Simon found means to ingratiate himself with Nero, the Roman Emperor; for Nero was, above all other mortals, infatuated with the superstitions of the black art to the last degree of folly and extravagance. To excel in this art was one of his greatest passions, and for this purpose he spared no expense and stuck at no crimes.

Simon Magus, then, by his vain boastings and illusions, could not fail to please this tyrant. The Fathers assure us that this famous magician had promised the Emperor and the people to fly in the air, carried by his angels, thus pretending to imitate the ascension of Christ. Accordingly, he raised himself in the air, by his magical power, in presence of the Emperor.

St. Peter and St. Paul, seeing the delusion, betook themselves to prayer, whereupon the devil lost his power, the impostor fell to the ground, was bruised, broke a leg, and died, a few days after, in rage and confusion.—(Butler's Lives of the Saints, vol. ii., pp. 348, 463, 464.)

I know a certain priest, who, one day, went to such a meeting with the intention of preventing the diabolical performances. He adjured the evil spirits not to exercise any influence, neither over their mediums, nor over any of those present at the meeting. What happened? It was in vain that the medium tried to make the spirits appear and speak. He told the assembly that the spirits would not come, that there must be some opposing power.

One day, the Earl of Fingal, in Ireland, Lord Plunket, father of Rev. Father Plunket, of the Congregation of the Most Holy Redeemer, happened to be present at a meeting of Spiritualists. The tables began to move. He became frightened, because he saw there was something preternatural in it. So he retired to a corner, and began to pray (to say the Rosary), and instantly the operations were stopped, and they could not get along any more, as long as he was there.—(Related by Father Phuket to one of our Fathers.)

The familiar spirits of spirit-mediums find an opposing power in the presence of sacred relics.

The Emperor Julian, surnamed the Apostate, was most foolishly superstitious, and exceedingly fond of soothsayers and magicians (or Spiritualists). Maximus, the Magician (or Spiritualist), and others of that character, were his chief confidants. He endeavored, by the black art, or by means of the devil, to rival the miracles of Christ, though he effected nothing.

At that time there was, at Daphne, five miles from Antioch, a famous idol of Apollo, which uttered oracles in that place. Gallus Cæsar, to oppose the worship of that idol, translated from Antioch to Daphne the sacred relies of St. Babylas, Bishop of Antioch, and Martyr. He erected a church, sacred to the name of St.

Babylas, near the profane temple (or devil's temple), and placed in it the venerable relics of the Martyr, in a shrine above ground. The neighborhood of the Martyr's relics struck the devil dumb. Eleven years after, Julian the Apostate came to Antioch, in the year 362, and, by a multitude of sacrifices, endeavored to learn of the idol the cause of his silence. At length the fiend gave him to understand that the neighborhood was full of dead bones, which must be removed before he could be at rest, and disposed to give answers. Julian understood this of the body of St. Babylas, and commanded that the Christians should immediately remove his shrine to some distant place, but not touch the other dead bodies. The Christians obeyed the order, and, with great solemnity, carried in procession the sacred relics back to Antioch, singing, on this occasion, the psalms which ridicule the vanity and feebleness of idols, repeating after every verse: "May they who adore idols and glory in false gods blush with shame, and be covered with confusion." The following evening lightning fell on the Temple of Apollo, and reduced to ashes the idol and all its ornaments. (Butler's Lives of the Saints, vol. i pp. 107 and 112, note.)

Holy water, too, or anything else, blessed by the Church, is an opposing power for these spirits. At the time when some of our Fathers gave a Mission in Erie, a meeting of Spiritualists was held in that city. When the Bishop heard of it, he sent one of our Fathers to present the evil spirits from exercising their influence over their mediums. The Father went in disguise to the house where the meeting was to take place. He took with him a bottle of holy water. Before the performance began, the Father sprinkled the whole floor with holy water. The medium, a young woman, came on the stage, to get into a trance, but she could not succeed. They tried for about an hour, but got no answer. At last the performer, the medium, said: "Ladies and gentlemen, we have to give up tonight. There must be some opposing power, as the spirits do not appear and speak."

When General Lamoricière, Commander of the Pope's Army, and a very pious Catholic, came back from Italy, he happened to be present at a meeting of Spiritualists. He held in his hand a little crucifix, blessed by our Holy Father the Pope. Now, when they laid their hands on the table, and invoked the spirits, none of the spirits would come and answer. The medium then came and said: "Gentlemen, there must be someone among you who is averse to the spirits." He examined the hands of every one, and found the little crucifix in the hand of General Lamoricière. He then told the General either to give up this article or to leave. The General left, the opposing power was gone, and the spirits could work through their medium.

Even the simple Sign of the Cross is an opposing power.

One day, as St. Gregory Thaumaturgus (worker of wonders) was returning from the city of Neocæsarea to the wilderness, a violent rain obliged him to take shelter in a heathenish temple, the most famous in the country, on account of oracles and divinations delivered there. At his entrance, he made the sign of the cross several times, to purify the air from the evil spirits, and then passed the night there with his companion in prayer, according to custom. The next morning he pursued his journey, and the idolatrous priest performed his usual superstitions in the temple; but the devils declared they could stay there no longer, being forced away by the man who had passed the night there. After several vain attempts to bring those powers back, the priest hastened after the saint, threatening to carry his complaints against him to the magistrates and to the Emperor. Gregory, without the least emotion, told him that, with the help of God, he could drive away or call the devils when he pleased. When the idolater saw that Gregory disregarded all his menaces, and when he heard that the saint had the power of commanding demons at pleasure, his fury was turned into admiration, and he entreated the Bishop, as a further evidence of the divine authority, to bring the demons back again to the temple. The saint complied with his request, and dismissed him with a scrip of paper on which he had written, "Gregory to Satan: Enter." This being laid upon the altar, and the usual oblation made, the demons gave their answers as usual. The priest, surprised at what he saw, went after the holy Bishop, and begged he would give him some account of that God whom his gods so readily obeyed. After being instructed in the principles of our holy religion, he renounced his devilish practices, and became a Christian. (Butler's Lives of the Saints, vol. iv., p. 356.)

Some time ago the Davenport brothers put up a blasphemous placard all over the city of St. Louis, Mo., informing the public that they could perform miracles similar to those of Christ. A certain priest of the city read this placard, and became quite indignant at it. He determined to expose the authors of the placard, so he went, in disguise, to the meeting. Now when they were about to perform their lying miracles, they put out the lights, and told all present to join hands and form a circle. The priest said to his neighbor: "I will not join hands with you, I wish to find out whether the joining of hands is necessary to the performance." As soon as the lights were put out, they heard music over their heads.

All went on very well. The priest saw that the circle was not necessary to the performance; that it was nothing but a cheat to make the affair mysterious. Having found this out, the priest made the sign of the cross. Instantly there was heard a shriek, and a crash. The lights were lit. Davenport came and said, "Gentlemen, some one of you must have broken the circle; please join hands once more, and do not break the circle." The lights were then put out again. The priest did not join hands with his neighbor, yet the performance went on well again as before. The priest again made the sign of the cross, and again there was heard a shriek and a crash. Davenport came down and complained. The priest's neighbor then cried out: "My neighbor here did not join hands with me." Every one shouted: "Put him out! put him out!" and Davenport, too, begged him to leave. But the priest, who was a strong man, said: "I will not leave until the performance is over. You will have some trouble and difficulty in putting me out; I have paid for my ticket, and I have as much right to stay as anyone else."

They could no longer succeed in the performance of their lying wonders. Everyone left; the priest stayed until all were gone. Davenport complained to him, saying: "Why did you act thus, and stop our proceedings?" "Well!" said the priest, "do you know who I am? I am a Catholic priest. I suppose you never had a Catholic priest in any of your circles. As you blasphemed God by your placard, I will expose you in all the newspapers of the city. A simple sign of the cross, which I made, was more powerful than all your evil spirits. Had they any power, they would have told you what was the opposing power." Davenport left next day. (St. Louis Guardian.)

Now every Christian knows that good angels or spirits are not afraid of, nor driven away by, prayer, by holy relics, by the sign of the cross, by holy water, or the like. It is only the devil who fears the power of prayer, and trembles in the presence of sacred objects, because he finds in them the power of Jesus Christ. It is, then, evident from these facts that spiritism is nothing but satanism.

VI

Holy Scripture tells us that Spiritualism is an abomination in the sight of God. Holy Scripture, it is true, does not use the word Spiritualism or Spiritism, but it uses another word which has the same meaning. Holy Scripture forbids necromancy, or the evocation of the dead, and commands that necromancers shall be put to death.

Now our modern Spiritualists openly assert that they hold intercourse with the spirits of the departed. They are, then, real necromancers, real diviners, attempting, by means of evoking the dead, to divine secrets, whether of the past or the future, unknown to the living. They practice what the world has always called divination, and that species of divination called necromancy. Thus far all is plain, certain, undeniable; and therefore they do that which the Christian world has always held to be unlawful, and a dealing with the devils.

VII

Modern Spiritualism is but a revival of the old heathen idol-worship.

Satan is constantly engaged in doing all in his power to entice men away from God, and to have himself worshiped instead of the Creator. The introduction, establishment, persistence and power, of the various cruel, filthy, and revolting superstitious of the ancient heathen world, or of pagan nations in modern times, are nothing but the work of the devil. They reveal a more than human power. God permitted Satan to operate upon man's morbid nature, as a deserved punishment upon the Gentiles for their hatred of truth, and their apostasy from the primitive religion. Men left to themselves, to human nature alone, however low they might be prone to descend, never could descend so low as to worship wood and stone, four-footed beasts and creeping things. To do this needs satanic delusion.

Paganism in its old form was doomed. Christianity had silenced the oracles, and driven the devils back to hell. How was the devil to reestablish his worship on earth, and carry on his war against the Son of God, and the religion which He taught us? Evidently only by changing his tactics and turning the truth into a lie. He found men in all the heresiarchs, who, like Eve, gave ear to his suggestions, and believed him more than the Infallible Word of Jesus Christ. Thus he has succeeded in banishing the true religion from whole countries, or in mixing it with false doctrines. He has prevailed upon thousands to believe the doctrines of vain, self-conceited men, rather than the religion taught by Jesus Christ and his Apostles. It is by heresies, revolutions, bad secret societies, and godless State school education, that he has succeeded so far as to bring thousands of men back to a state of heathenism and infidelity. The time has come for him to introduce idolatry or his own worship. To do this he makes use of spiritualism. Through the spirit-mediums he performs lying wonders. He gives pretended revelations from the spirit world, in order to destroy or weaken all faith in divine revelation. He thus strives to reestablish in Christian lands that very same devil-worship which has so long existed among heathen nations, and which our Lord Jesus Christ came to destroy. The Holy Scriptures assure us that all the gods of the heathens are devils. ("Omnes dii gentium daemonia."—Ps.) These demons took possession of the idols made of wood or stone, of gold or silver; they had temples erected in their honor; they had their sacrifices, their priests and their priestesses. They uttered oracles. They were consulted through their medium's in all affairs of importance, and especially in order to find out the future, precisely as they are consulted by our modern Spiritualists at the present day.

That God has severely punished those who hold dealings and communications with the devil, we find recorded in Holy Scriptures. In the Book of Kings, we are told that when Ochozias, King of Israel, fell sick, he sent to Accaron, to consult the god of the Philistines about his health, but Elias the Prophet came to him, in the name of God, and told him that he would not rise again from his sick bed, because he had, through spirit-mediums, consulted Beelzebub, the god of Accaron.

King Saul was slain in battle because he had recourse to a witch, i.e., a spirit-medium.

Holy Scripture also tells how King Achab consulted the false prophets, or spirit-mediums, and how God gave power to the devil to deceive these mediums, and tell falsehoods to the King. Achab believed them, and God punished him; for, soon after, the King perished in battle.

The same kind of death was inflicted upon the Emperor Julian, who was so fond of consulting the devil by his mediums.

In our own days we see similar punishments inflicted upon those who practice spiritualism, and even on those who take but a slight part in it.

I know a certain doctor who assisted sometimes, out of curiosity, at these diabolical circles of Spiritualists.

When he came to understand that it was sinful to assist at such meetings even from a spirit of curiosity, he never went again; but he was punished for having entered the house of the devil. He came to me, and told me how he was harassed and tormented every night by evil spirits, that they made a horrible noise in his room, and prevented him from sleeping.

"I would not care for the noise," said he, "provided I could sleep, but I have not slept for several weeks, and I am so nervous and excited that I cannot bear it any longer; I shall become insane if it continues so any longer. Please, Father, help me if you can."

I told him to kneel down, and I recited over him the prayers prescribed by the Catholic Church for such persons. The evil spirits left him quiet for about a month, when they began again to disturb him during the night. The doctor came again to me, that I might pray over him. I did so, and the evil spirits retired again. This happened about four years ago.

Last summer I saw the doctor, and asked him whether the evil spirits had left him alone. He said: "Yes, I have not suffered any more from them since I saw you last."

This is an instance of but a slight punishment; but there are on record instances of far severer punishments.

Experience teaches that those who practice Spiritualism often turn insane in the end, and become perfect maniacs.

You have, probably, read of many such cases of insanity in the newspapers. The Boston Pilot writes, Jan. 1, 1852: "Most mediums become misanthropical, idiotic, or insane. The same happens even to many of the auditors. Experience teaches that, almost every week, one of these unfortunate persons commits suicide, or is locked up in a mad-house. Many of these mediums betray evident signs of mental derangement, and even sometimes not less evident marks of satanic possession."

The Courier and Inquirer writes, May 10, 1852, that, in the month of April, in Indiana, six persons were taken to the insane asylum in consequence of the intercourse which they had held with spirit-rappers.

The Herald mentions, under date of April 30, 1852, that Mr. Junius Alcott, of Utica, committed suicide in a fit of insanity brought on by the same cause.

In Paris, in the same year, many persons, while taking part in table-rapping, suddenly became insane, and found their way to the mad-house in Bicetre and Charenton, and others were taken to private insane institutions.

Madame Victoria d'Hennequin also died insane. Her husband, too, died a maniac; he had discharged the office of secretary to the spirit of the earth, which communicated with him through the medium of a small table. Not long ago a certain person of Pittsburgh, and some others of Philadelphia, who made frequent use of the planchette, became insane, and were put in the insane asylum.

Another famous Spiritualist, of Philadelphia, committed suicide because the spirit told him to do so.

It would take me too long to adduce more instances of this kind, to show how the votaries of spiritualism are punished even in this life. What I have said on spiritualism, should be sufficient to convince every sincere mind that the Catholic Church is right in condemning as unlawful the practice of spiritualism.

In the admirable book of the Council of Baltimore—lately published—which it is enjoined on all, Bishops, Priests, and Laity, to observe strictly, after a brief exposition of the rogueries of Magnetism, Clairvoyance, and Spiritism, as part foolery and part an open door to deviltry, the Fathers of the Council, as approved at Rome, conclude by saying:

"It is a great solace to us that our children, beloved in Christ, the Catholic faithful, have not, thus far, been infected with this plague. And we exhort them, in the Lord, that they never give countenance to spiritism, even in the most casual manner; and that they do not, through any curiosity, ever be present at its Circles. For they who enter the house of the devil, have all reason to fear that they will be deluded by his devices, and enslaved to his command. Against the vile snares of these people, the Apostle, inspired by the Holy Ghost, spoke in prophecy of these last days of the world: the Spirit speaketh, openly, that in the last days some will fall away from the Faith, adhering to spirits of error, and to doctrines of devils, in hypocrisy speaking falsehood, and having their conscience seared."—Tit. I., p. 33.

The claims of Spiritualism are very high, but there is abundant proof to show that, instead of being "ancient Christianity revived," it is, perhaps, the worst enemy that Christianity ever had to meet. It is Satan's last grand effort to substitute his own infernal worship for the worship of God. The snares of the devil are cunningly laid. Thousands and millions are already his deluded victims. Occasionally we hear a warning voice from one who has escaped from his power, like a mariner from the sinking wreck; but the greater part of Satan's deluded followers, after they have been once initiated into the Spiritualist "Circle," are like boatmen in the midst of a terrible whirlpool—their destruction is inevitable!

Mr. J. F. Whitney, editor of the "New York Pathfinder," was formerly a warm advocate of Spiritualism, and published much in its favor. Hear what he says:

"Now after long and constant watchfulness, after seeing for months and years the progress and practical workings of Spiritualism upon its devotees and its mediums, we are compelled to speak our honest conviction, that the manifestations coming through the acknowledged mediums, whether rapping, tipping, writing, or entranced mediums, have a baneful influence upon its followers, and create discord and confusion. The generality of their teachings inculcate false ideas, and uphold principles and theories which, when carried out, debase men and make them little better than the brute…"

"We have seen the gradual progress it makes with its believers, and particularly its mediums, from morality to sensuality and immorality. We have seen it gradually undermining the foundation of good principles—we have noticed with amazement the radical change which a few months will bring about in individuals.

We desire," he says in conclusion, "to send forth our warning voice; and if our position as head of a public journal, our known advocacy of Spiritualism, our experience, and the conspicuous part we have played among its believers, the honesty and fearlessness with which we have defended the subject, will weigh anything in our favor, we desire that our opinions may be received; we desire that those who are moving passively down the rushing rapids to destruction, should pause—ere it be too late—and save themselves from the blasting influence which these manifestations are causing."

THE END.